Kon Hwon Yang

P9-DTE-311

THE TWELVE MINOR PROPHETS

Rev. GEORGE L. ROBINSON, Ph.D., D.D., LL.D.

THE TWELVE
MINOR PROPHETS

BY

Rev. GEORGE L. ROBINSON, PH.D., D.D., LL.D.

PROFESSOR OF BIBLICAL LITERATURE AND ENGLISH BIBLE McCORMICK
THEOLOGICAL SEMINARY, CHICAGO, ILLINOIS

NEW YORK
GEORGE H. DORAN COMPANY

THE TWELVE MINOR PROPHETS
— A —
PRINTED IN THE UNITED STATES OF AMERICA

PREFACE

This little handbook is intended to assist Bible study classes wishing to become acquainted with the times and teachings of the Twelve Minor Prophets. It is the product of not only one or two, but of several years' experience in teaching; growing at the rate of one, or at most two, chapters a year, out of a somewhat careful examination of the original text. This was John Milton's way of writing a book! The author's aim has been two-fold: first, to present the wonderful messages of these immortal preachers in their own historical setting and environment; and, second, to emphasize their permanent value to the world of to-day. Their Oriental coloring has been observed and annotated frequently, and their style, rhythm and metre have not been entirely ignored.

No claim is laid to originality except that which a sympathetic interpreter naturally puts upon his own work. The author has avoided the extreme positions either of tradition or criticism. For, while he believes that the Twelve were inspired with visions of the Messiah and of the Messianic age, yet he does not find that they so completely unfolded revelations of the Christ and of Messianic bliss as to render the advent of the Messiah unnecessary; and, on the other hand, though the earlier pre-exilic prophets were emphatic in denouncing Israel's sins, yet he believes that they did not confine themselves to censure or condemnation, as so many claim, "without promising one word of consolation"! The truth rather lies between such extremes. With God judgment and mercy are close allies. As Melville Scott says, in his somewhat exceptionally sane monograph on *The Message of Hosea,* "Reverence has not always been critical, and criticism has not always been reverent. What is needed is to combine the tone and temper of the old school with the more scientific methods of the new, and both schools will be bettered by the fusion." This has long been the conviction of the present author. While he acknowledges great indebtedness to his predecessors, he has carefully presented only the interpretations and opinions, which, after reflection, he has made his own.

CONTENTS

LITERATURE ON
THE TWELVE MINOR PROPHETS

International Critical Commentary (1905-12);
G. A. Smith, "The Twelve Prophets," *Expositor's
Bible* (1896-98); *The Cambridge Bible for Schools
and Colleges* (1884 ff.); *The New Century Bible,*
"The Minor Prophets"; E. B. Pusey, *The Minor
Prophets, with a Commentary Explanatory and
Practical* (1885); J. Calvin, *Commentary on the
Twelve Minor Prophets* (Eng. transl., 1846); Wil-
liams, *The Minor Prophets Unfolded* (1919); E.
Henderson, *The Book of the Twelve Minor Pro-
phets* (1868); J. M. P. Smith, *The Prophets and
their Times* (1925); J. R. Dummelow, *The One
Volume Bible Commentary* (1909); A. S. Peake, *A
Commentary on the Bible* (1919); *Ibid., The Roots
of Hebrew Prophecy and Jewish Apocalyptic*
(1923); Theodore of Mopsuestia, *Commentary on
the Twelve Prophets,* edited by W. C. H. toe Water
under the title *Specimen observationum de Theo-
doro . . . XII prophetarum minorum interprete*
(Amsterdam, 1837); F. W. Farrar, "The Minor
Prophets, their lives and times," *Men of the Bible*
(1890); F. C. Eiselen, *The Minor Prophets*
(1907); T. H. Robinson, *Prophecy and the Prophets* (1923); C. von Orelli, *Ezekiel und die kleinen
Propheten* (1896; translated by J. S. Banks, 1893);
C. F. Keil, *Die kleinen Propheten* (translated,

1888); E. Reuss, *La Bible II* (1876); F. Hitzig, *Die kleinen Propheten* (revised by H. Steiner, 1881); H. Ewald, *Die Propheten des Alten Bundes* (1867); J. Wellhausen, *Die kleinen Propheten übersetzst und erklärt* (1898); B. Duhm, *Die zwölf Propheten in den Versmassen der Urschrift* (1910; translated by Archibald Duffy 1912); *Anmerkungen zu den zwölf Propheten* (1911); *Israels Propheten* (1916); G. Richter, *Erläuterungen zu dunklen Stellen in den kleinen Propheten* (1914); Arnold B. Ehrlich, *Randglossen zur hebräischen Bibel* (1912); G. Hölscher, *Die Propheten* (1914); O. Procksch, *Die kleinen prophetischen Schriften* (1916); W. Nowack, "Die kleinen Propheten übersetzt und erklärt." *Göttinger Handkommentar zum A. T.* (1922); K. Marti, "Dodeka-propheton," *Kurzer Handkommentar zum A. T.* (1904); A. Hoonacker, *Les douze petits Prophètes* (1908); E. Sellin, *Das Zwölfprophetenbuch übersetzt und erklärt* (1922).

CHRONOLOGICAL TABLE

B. C.

ca. 930,	Schism between Israel and Judah.
" 800,	(or, toward close of 9th century) Joel.
" 760,	Amos.
" 750–25,	Hosea.
" 750,	(or, shortly after 750) Nahum.
" 734–2,	First decimation of North Israel by Assyria.
" 725–15,	Micah.
" 722,	Downfall of North Israel.
" 700,	(or, at latest, before Jeremiah) Obadiah.
" 700–600,	The Book of Jonah.
" 625,	Zephaniah.
" 621',	Discovery of the Book of the Law.
" 603,	Habakkuk.
" 597,	First captivity of Judah by Nebuchadnezzar.
" 586,	Final Downfall of Jerusalem.
" 536,	Return of the Jews under Zerubbabel and Joshua.
" 520,	Haggai.
" 520–16,	Zechariah.
" 516,	Dedication of the Second Temple.
" 458,	Return of Ezra.
" 445,	First return of Nehemiah.
" 444,	The Law read and expounded by Ezra.
" 432,	Second return of Nehemiah.
" 445–432,	Malachi.
" 333,	Alexander the Great.
" 167–164,	Maccabean Uprising.

THE TWELVE MINOR PROPHETS

THE TWELVE MINOR PROPHETS

CHAPTER I

HOSEA THE PROPHET OF LOVE

I. *Name and Personality.*—The name Hosea, like
that of Joshua and Jesus, which spring from the
same root, signifies "salvation," "help," "deliverance." Very probably the prophet was a native of
North Israel, as his frequent allusions to Lebanon,
Tabor, Samaria, Bethel, Jezreel and Ramah would
imply. Of "Ephraim" alone he speaks some thirty-
seven times. "In every sentence," says Ewald, "it
appears that Hosea had not only visited the kingdom of Ephraim, as Amos had done, but that he is
acquainted with it from the depths of his heart, and
follows all its doings, aims, and fortunes with the
profound feelings gendered of such a sympathy as is
conceivable in the case of a native prophet only."
As a son of the soil he drew many of his simple and
charming images from the fireside, the garden, and
the farm (4:16; 7:4-8; 8:7; 10:11; 11:4; 13:3,
15; 14:7). In this he stands in contrast with Amos,
who reflects the desert mountains of Judah and the
Dead Sea. Hosea was the home missionary of
North Israel, as Jonah was their foreign. He was
gentle, pensive, and inclined to melancholy, but
frank, affectionate, and full of domestic feeling. He

was the Jeremiah of the northern kingdom, and, like him, was little less than a martyr, prefiguring Christ. Both were ardent patriots, possessed of finely sensitive religious natures. Jeremiah was the more studied and self-conscious in his grief; Hosea, the more artless and passionate. Jeremiah was more of a theologian; Hosea, more of a poet. His book is both a prophecy and a poem; one of the most difficult, but at the same time one of the most evangelical of the Old Testament. This is due not to any special Messianic predictions enunciated, but because he announced centuries in advance "the new commandment" of the Gospels, and was the first of the seers to grasp the truth that God is love, and that Israel's sin of sins was not to have recognized the love of God. Hosea was thus the St. John of the Old Testament.

II. *His Times.*—The title to his Book reads, "The word of Jehovah that came unto Hosea, the son of Beeri, in the days of Uzziah, Jotham, Ahaz, and Hezekiah, kings of Judah, and in the days of Jeroboam, the son of Joash, king of Israel" (1:1). Accordingly, Hosea, like Amos, began preaching in times of great prosperity, and left off when the nation was struggling in the grip of anarchy! During his earlier years Jeroboam II was the *grand monarque,* the Louis XIV of Samaria. He stood at the head of an arrogant military despotism—a true descendant of Jehu! In his day the nation was at the summit of its military prosperity, but, at the same time, far down the slope of a fatal moral declension. The Second Book of Kings informs us that upon the death of Jeroboam, internal feuds took place, rival politicians sacrificed the nation's interests

to their own, princes became debauched, phantom
kings were set up, and the national power became
seriously weakened. Kings were cut off "as foam
upon the water" (Hos. 10:7). Jeroboam was the
last really strong man of Israel. Of the six kings
who succeeded him only Menahem died a natural
death. "Conspiracy" is the keyword of the history
of the period (cf. II Kings 15). Zechariah reigned
six months; Shallum, only one. In their desperation,
accordingly, they leaned first one way and then another to secure foreign help, paying tribute alter-
nately to Assyria and to Egypt, until they finally
lost their independence and national autonomy, exhausted their energies and resources, and were
forced to accept of abject vassalage to Assyria.
Their decline was rapid as soon as their independence was gone. To a patriot like Hosea, it was
terrible to appeal to foreign governments for help
(8:9, 10:6). Such a policy was no remedy for the
nation's moral disease (5:13). Unconsciously Ephraim became prematurely old. "Gray hairs" were
here and there upon him and he knew it not (7:9).
All classes of society became demoralized. Even the
priests turned bandit and rejoiced in the sins of the
people, because it increased their revenues. Things
went from bad to worse, until the prophet exclaimed,
"There is no truth, nor goodness, nor knowledge of
God in the land. There is naught but swearing and
breaking faith, and killing, and stealing, and commit-
ting adultery; they break out and blood toucheth
blood" (4:1, 2). The conditions were terrible! Religion sank into the most sensual idolatry. Family
life, especially, became dissolute. Upon it, accordingly, the prophet laid his heaviest indictment. To

express their hopeless condition he uses the hateful word "whoredom" some sixteen times. As Davidson says, "Hosea lived during, perhaps, the most unquiet and turbulent times through which the country had ever passed." The fury of the various factions was like raging heat: "They are as an oven heated by the baker" (7:4). Men everywhere were pitted against each other. The outlook was hopeless. Israel's sun was setting. It hardly needed a prophet to discern that the end of the State was near. It was not long indeed after Hosea ceased to preach that they were carried away by Sargon into captivity to Assyria, B. C., 722 (II Kings 17).

III. *The Duration of Hosea's Ministry.*—Some assign but a brief period of about ten years to Hosea's active ministry. This conclusion is based upon the prophet's references to "Gilead" in 6:8 and 12:11, which seem to indicate that Hosea was ignorant of the Syro-Ephraimitic War (B. C. 734). But more recently Alt has pointed out that 5:8-6:3 definitely refer to this war. Besides, the rôle played by the Egyptians in 7:11; 9:3, 6; 11:5; 12:1, as the counterpoise to Assyria seems, as Sellin observes, to take us down to the time of Hoshea, the last king of the northern kingdom. Add to this the prophet's allusion in 10:14 to Shalman's capture of Beth-arbel, and this brings him down to 725 B. C., for it was probably in that year that Shalmanezer IV (who is best identified with Shalman) took Beth-arbel. According to II Kings 17:3, 4, Shalmanezer made two invasions into Canaan: the first, when he took Beth-arbel and imposed tribute on North Israel, and the second, which he undertook because King Hoshea had broken the terms agreed

upon. Wellhausen, Nowack, and others, on the contrary, deny the genuineness of Hos. 10:14. For, like
Eiselen, they reason, "If the allusion in 10:14 is to
Shalmanezer IV the passage must be a later addition,
since Hosea's activity ended before this king as-
cended the throne." But it is better, with Davidson,
to allow that Hosea's prophecies "extended over a
considerable period of Israel's history." Person-
ally we would assign him to the years between 750
and 725 B. C. In this Sellin also concurs.

IV. *Hosea's Call* (Chaps. 1-3).—Hosea's personal history, which he interpreted as a symbol of
Jehovah's experience with Israel, may be regarded
as the master-key of his teaching. Delicately and
without self-consciousness he tells the tragic story of
his domestic life. It burned two ideas into his soul:
Jehovah's loving faithfulness to Israel, and Israel's
thankless unfaithfulness to Jehovah. "When Jehovah spake at the first by Hosea, Jehovah said unto
Hosea, Go take unto thee a wife of whoredom and
children of whoredom" (1:2). The woman he
chose was Gomer, who bore him two sons and one
daughter; a son, Jezreel, "Vengeance"; a daughter,
Lo-ruhamah, "Uncompassionated"; and a son, Lo-
ammi, "Not my people"; their names pointing sig-
nificantly to the judgments which would inevitably
descend upon the house of Jehu. Gomer proved
faithless to her marriage vows; becoming ensnared
by the wild orgies of Baal and Ashtaroth, she de-
serted her husband for a paramour and fell into sensual slavery. But Hosea redeemed her for fifteen
silverlings and a homer and a half of barley (3:2);
thus from the bitterness of his own home trials the
prophet learned of the unquenchable love of Jeho-

vah. The whole account bears the stamp of reality;
indeed, only as real history would the prophet's
words have any effect. For, his domestic experience
served as a living mirror of Israel's unfaithful relation to Jehovah. It is useless to object to the literal
interpretation of these chapters; for, if they are to
be taken as figurative or allegorical only, such an
interpretation would reflect upon the prophet's
actual wife, if he were married; or, upon the prophet
himself, if unmarried. The whole story, including
chap. 3, is one piece; chaps. 1 and 3 referring to the
same woman, and to the same command of Jehovah
to Hosea to marry a harlot. Such a thought is aw-
fully repulsive to our modern sense, still more to
the mind of the ancient Hebrews. By many it is
assumed that Gomer was a pure woman up until the
time of her marriage, with only latent tendencies to
an immoral life. So taught Ambrose, Theodoret,
Cyril of Alexandria, and Theodore of Mopsuestia.
Not that Hosea, "with his eyes wide open," married a woman who was already "of evil reputation,"
as J. M. P. Smith and others aver; for, as Davidson points out, "to suppose that Jehovah would
have commanded his prophet to ally himself to a
woman already known as of impure life is absurd
and monstrous!" In any case we have an instance
of a bad wife who made a good prophet! But
what if Gomer were originally a sacred prostitute?
—"a holy woman," as T. H. Robinson suggests,
(for the Hebrew word for "harlot" and "holy
woman" is one and the same)—a woman whom the
prophet purchased from the shrine to which she was
attached? Sacramental fornication was a normal
feature of polytheistic religions, based on nature

worship. It is so in India today; and it was so in Græco-Roman religion influenced as it was by Asiatic cults. It is not impossible, therefore, that a sort of religious sanctity attached to such a marriage, and, that Hosea's action was regarded, indeed, as lawful and even meritorious. In any case Hosea's choice of Gomer presents a problem in the Divine Providence which finds a parallel only in Jesus' choice of Judas Iscariot. Surely, there may have been one exception of sexual immorality which was palliated by the people and condoned by Jehovah! Such a theory helps to explain the psychology of Hosea's religious development. In all the world's literature there is no record of human love like that of Hosea. His passion for Gomer was no mere explosive flash of strong emotion; rather it was a consuming fire, shut up in his bones, which no infidelity on her part could weaken, or personal suffering on his part could quench. Through her treacherous rejection of his affection and loyalty, Hosea discovered there was no true love apart from pain; and conversely, also, that there is no real pain without love. He is, therefore, appropriately called "the Minnesinger among the Prophets!"

V. *Hosea's Message* (Chaps. 4-14).—Analysis of Hosea's book is well-nigh impossible; yet it bears throughout a distinctly personal stamp, being probably the carefully collected "notes" of many years. Very appropriately it has been described as "one long impassioned monologue, broken by sobs"; or, as Kautzsch puts it, "more sob than speech." This much is clear: Chaps. 1-3 tell of the messenger; while chaps. 4-14 tell of his message. The first section is a sort of spiritual autobiography, half narrative, half prophecy, the *confessio amantis*, wrung from a heart which through the anguish of outraged human love has won its way into the secret of the love divine. The second section consists of a series of homilies, mere fragments of warning and promise, without any clearly articulated divisions. The reason for this mixed and desultory type of prophetic utterance is perfectly clear, however, when we reflect that Hosea's theology is the theology of the heart rather than of the head. Various attempts have been made to trace a chronological sequence in the excerpts of chaps. 4-14; thus Ewald thought he had discovered even an artistic poetic arrangement: (1) 4:1—6: 11a, the arraignment: (2) 6:11b—9:9, the punishment; and (3) 9:10—14:9, retrospect of Israel's earlier history, exhortation and comfort. In a similar way Kirkpatrick made a three-fold subdivision: (1) 4-8, Israel's guilt; (2) 9:1—11:11, Israel's doom; (3) 11:12—14:9, Israel's retrospect and prospect. But it is better to allow that the great ideas of the prophet's preaching being limited in number were oft repeated, and that order and sequence are almost ignored. As a matter of fact, the salient teachings of his entire book may be summed up under the three words complaint, condemnation, and consolation; the only progress of thought discernible being that of a general advance from (1) Israel's guilt, to that (2) of punishment, and (3) of final restoration. There is a monotony of grief throughout the book, as there is in the "Lamentations of Jeremiah," which is uttered in different varieties of phrase and cadence, causing a heart-moving effect. Nevertheless, it is possible to trace, for homi-

letic purposes, the successive steps in Israel's national
downfall, as follows:

1. *Lack of knowledge.*—"My people are destroyed for lack of knowledge" (4:6); i. e., for
lack of *head!* This is Hosea's fundamental charge.
The nation is ignorant of God's law. The people
are simply stupid, they have no brains; "whoredom
and wine and new wine take away the brains" (4:
11)—"heart" in Hebrew being equivalent to the
English word "brains." Thus the prophet's fundamental rebuke is an intellectual one.

2. *Pride.*—"And the pride of Israel doth testify
to his face" (5:5); i. e., Israel has a diseased *heart!*
They were not only patriotic but arrogant. Ephraim
strove to rival the heathen as a world power. Jeroboam's prosperity was proving a snare. National
honor was becoming synonymous with national
whoredom! One is reminded in this connection of
the minatory words of James Russell Lowell on the
occasion of the two hundred and fiftieth anniversary
of Harvard University. He says:

"I am saddened when I see our success as a nation
measured by the number of acres under tillage, or of
bushels of wheat exported, for the real value of a
country must be weighed in scales more delicate than
the balance of trade. The gardens of Sicily are
empty now, but the bees of all climes still fetch
honey from the tiny garden plot of Theocritus. On
a map of the world you may cover Judæa with your
thumb, Athens with a finger tip, and neither of them
figures in the prices current; but they still live in the
thought and action of every civilized man. Did not
Dante cover with his hood all that was in Italy six
hundred years ago? And if we go back a century,

where was Germany unless in Weimar? Material success is good, but only as the necessary preliminary of better things. The measure of a nation's true success is the amount it has contributed to the thought, the moral energy, the intellectual happiness, the spiritual hope and consolation of mankind."

3. *Instability.*—"For your goodness is as a morning cloud, or as the dew that goeth early away" (6:4); i. e., *life* is stifled by hypocrisy and ritual! Goodness had lost its virtue. Worship which ought to have been spiritual had become formal and stereotyped: "For I desired goodness and not sacrifice, and the knowledge of God more than burnt offerings" (6:6).

4. *Worldliness.*—"Ephraim, he mixeth himself among the peoples; Ephraim is a cake not turned" (7:8); i. e., the nation's *politics* were bad! Ephraim, like a silly dove, without understanding, sought alliances with Egypt and Assyria, thus coquetting with Jehovah. The nation, however, had been strenuously enjoined by the great law-giver to remain separate from other peoples. Besides, Ephraim was a cake not turned, "a charred scone," half raw on one side, half a cinder on the other! Some too rich, others too poor! hot in politics, cold in religion! The extremes of society being too great!

5. *Corruption.*—"They have deeply corrupted themselves as in the days of Gibeah" (9:9); i. e., their *religion* was rotten! Corruption in politics was bad enough, but in religion it was unpardonable. Phœnician and Canaanite nature-worship was unspeakably immoral. Israel were playing the harlot under the cloak of religion: they went to Baalpeor (9:10).

6. *Backsliding.*—"My people are bent on backsliding from me" (11:7); i. e., backsliding had become a habit! Men were perishing because of their own wicked counsels (11:6); the Nemesis of evil being wrapped up in itself. Yet Jehovah still loves Israel and longs to save them: "How shall I give thee up Ephraim? how shall I cast thee off, Israel?" (11:8). For, though Israel had contracted the habit of backsliding, Jehovah was still willing to continue the Divine pursuit (cf. Ps. 23:6).

7. *Idolatry.*—"And now they sin more and more, and have made them molten images of their silver, even idols, according to their own understanding" (13:2); i. e., they had become guilty of *complete abandon!* No prophet ever scorned more sincerely than Hosea a manufactured God; he traced, indeed, as we have seen, all of Israel's sins back to infidelity to God.

These to Hosea were seven of the principal steps in Israel's downfall, which led straight to the precipice of national ruin! But the prophet's book does not close without a gracious offer of forgiveness (chap. 14). Though Israel stands guilty before Jehovah, yet, through repentance, restoration is not impossible: "O Israel, return unto Jehovah thy God; for thou hast fallen by thine iniquity. Take with you words, and return unto Jehovah: say unto Jehovah, Take away all iniquity" (14: 1, 2). He will graciously respond, "I will heal their backsliding, I will love them freely; for mine anger is turned away from him" (14:4). Ephraim has still one more chance. Love must prevail; for love is greater than Law. "If he sin against law he will be maimed; if he sin against love he will be lost." Mercy must

triumph over judgment. Thus Hosea has the same
message in essence as Amos, only he carries it deeper,
lodging it in the love of God.   Hosea is distinctively
the prophet of grace. He anticipated, and in a very
true sense prepared for Calvary. "Come back," he
pleads, "Come back; if you only knew how God loves
you, you would come back. Take with you words
and pray, and God will receive you graciously." And
so he finally concludes in an epilogue which sums
up his entire message: "Who is wise, that he may
understand these things? prudent that he may know
them? for the ways of Jehovah are right, and the
just shall walk in them; but transgressors shall fall
therein" (14:9); which means, whoever desires to
become wise and prudent, let him acquaint himself
with these oracles, and from them learn: (1) that
Jehovah's ways are right, and (2) that the destinies
of men are determined by their attitude to the divine
will.

VI. *Hosea's Message to us.*—One general lesson
is taught by Hosea of ever permanent worth, namely,
that inward corruption in a nation is more dangerous
to its existence than their external enemies. And a
kindred lesson closely related to this is: that the
truest of all patriots is he who, like Hosea, identifies
himself with his people, sorrows over their calamities
as though they were his own, and repents for their
sins as though he had committed them himself. Hosea's message, accordingly, is not out of date. The
God *of* ancient history is a God *in* modern history.
All national events are still under the Divine super-
intendence. The God of Israel still chooses his
agents, both national and individual. This is the one

permanent lesson taught by Hosea.   Certain more specific lessons are the following:

1. The folly of sacrificing national interests to personal advantage (5:10, 11).

2. The penalty of condoning vice (4:13-19).

3. The rapid decline of a nation when the religious leaders become corrupt; "like people, like priest" (4:9).

4. The Nemesis of neglecting God's law (4:6; 8:1, 12).

5. God's fatherly desire to show mercy (*hesed*). This Hebrew word, which occurs so frequently in the book of Psalms, conveys a thought closely akin to "grace" in the New Testament.   It is used by Hosea six times (2:19; 4:1; 6:4; 6:6; 10:12; 12:6) being translated by "goodness," "kindness," and even "loving-kindness."   Hosea, accordingly, is correctly regarded as "the Prophet of Love."   Amos never employs the term.   To Hosea it meant what is usually conveyed by the Scotch term "leal-love," i. e., love plus loyalty, including both love for God and for our fellow-men.   Hosea was the evangelist of a new Gospel, "If Psalm 22 is the Calvary of the Old Testament, Hosea's sobs are its Gethsemane." Echoes of the prophet are found in the New Testament: thus, Hos. 11:1 in Matt. 2:15; Hos. 10:8 in Lk. 23:30; Hos. 2:23 in I Pet. 2:10; Hos. 6:6 in Matt. 9:13; 12:7.

VII. *Pemmican Passages in Hosea;* i. e., great texts, worthy of being masticated, digested, and remembered:

1. "For I desire goodness and not sacrifice"; (6:6)—a passage which had special attraction for Jesus (Matt. 9:13; 12:7).

2. "How shall I give thee up Ephraim? how shall I cast thee off Israel?" (11:8),—perhaps the most significant passage in the book!

3. "Let us follow on to know Jehovah" (6:3),— a very remarkable exhortation to spring from the eighth century B. C.!

4. "Ephraim is joined to idols; let him alone" (4:17),—lest contagion be contracted!

5. "Gray hairs are here and there upon him, and he knoweth it not" (7:9),—a rarely suggestive epigram!

6. "For they sow the wind, and they shall reap the whirlwind" (8:7),—anticipating Paul's exhortation to the Galatians (Gal. 6:7).

7. "I wrote for him the ten thousand things of my law; but they are counted a strange thing" (8:12), —from which it is justly inferred that already in Hosea's time a voluminous religious literature was in existence.

8. "Give them, O Jehovah: what wilt thou give? give them a miscarrying womb and dry breasts" (9: 14),—a strange imprecation to be found among the writings of "the prophet of love" (cf. Hos. 13: 14-16).

9. "They shall say to the mountains, Cover us; and to the hills, Fall on us" (10:8),—a graphic touch in the prophet's description of Samaria's ruin!

10. "It is time to seek Jehovah" (10:12),—applicable to all generations in all time!

11. "For I am God and not man; The Holy One in the midst of thee" (11:9),—therefore, free from all vengeance.

12. "Besides me there is no saviour" (13:4),— an oft recurring thought in Isaiah 40-66.

13. "Who is wise, that he may understand these things" (14:9),—a final sentence, which, like the concluding sentences of Ezekiel, Nahum, and Zephaniah, respectively, gathers up the spirit and teaching of the prophet's entire message.

14. Notable epigrams also: "Like people, like priest" (4:9); "Cut off as foam upon the water" (10:7); "drew them with cords of a man" (11:4); "I will be as the dew unto Israel" (14:5); "Ephraim is a cake not turned" (7:8).

SPECIAL LITERATURE ON HOSEA

Melville Scott, *The Message of Hosea* (1921); A. Tweedie, *A Sketch of Amos and Hosea,* their message and their times (1916); A. H. Sayce, "Hosea in the Light of Assyrian Research," *Jewish Quarterly Review* (1889); Articles on "Hosea" in *Dictionaries of the Bible, Encyclopædias,* etc.; also *Introductions to the Old Testament*: Driver, Cornill, Mackay, McFadyen, Moore, Gray, Raven, Wright, Sellin, and the collective work, entitled *Book by Book* (1896); W. Nowack, *Der Prophet Hosea Erklärt* (1880); A. Scholz, *Kommentar zum Buch des Propheten Hosea* (1882); Valeton, *Amos en Hosea* (1894), German translation by Echternacht (1898); Oettli, *Amos und Hosea* (1901); Volz, "Die Ehegeschichte Hoseas," ZWTh (1898), pp. 321-35; Baumgartner, *Kennen Amos und Hosea eine Heilseschatologie?* (1913); Peiser, *Hosea* (1914); Prätorius, *Bemerkungen zum Buch Hosea* (1918); Alt, "Hosea 5:8-6:6," *Neue kirchliche Zeitschrift* (1919), pp. 537-68.

CHAPTER II

JOEL THE PROPHET OF PENTECOST

I. *The Prophet's Personality.*—Nothing is known of Joel's birthplace or biography, his career and personality being shrouded in obscurity. Only a few inferences may be safely drawn from his writings. Such silence concerning God's spiritual agents is no uncommon occurrence in the Old Testament, for others are introduced in this semi-anonymous fashion; perhaps on purpose, that God himself, and not they, may have the glory. We are told, however, that the prophet was the son of Pethuel; the name being supposed to mean "Persuaded of God," (Joel 1:1; compare the reading "Bethuel" which occurs in both the Septuagint and Syriac Versions).

Joel's own name, in Hebrew *Yo-el,* signifies "Jehovah is God," and therefore, like the name "Micah," seems to enshrine in it a brief confession of faith, reflecting possibly the piety of his godly parents. The name occurs frequently in the Old Testament, there being at least a dozen other men who bore the same: for example, Joel, the elder son of Samuel and father of Heman the singer (I Sam. 8:2; I Chron. 6:33), and Joel, one of David's valiant men, and brother of Nathan (I Chron. 11:38).

It is probable that the prophet was a native of Judah, perhaps a citizen of Jerusalem, as he speaks familiarly of "Zion" and "the children of Zion" (2:1, 23), of "Judah and Jerusalem", and of "the children of Judah and the children of Jerusalem" (3:1, 6). From his interest in the Temple, it has been inferred also that he was a priest (1:13-17). In any case, from his prophecies it is very evident that he was not only a poet and a man of prayer, but a seer and a prophet in the strictest sense; for, he preached repentance with divine emphasis, and announced (he being perhaps the first to do so) the coming of the great and terrible "day of Jehovah" (2:11, 31). He may even have belonged to the guilds known in early Hebrew history as "the sons of the prophets."

II. *Outline and Contents.*—There are but two main divisions to Joel's book: (1) chaps. 1:2—2:17 (thirty-seven verses), in which the prophet speaks; describing most graphically in the first instance a plague of locusts accompanied by drought, and closing with an earnest exhortation to repentance; and (2) 2:18—3:21 (thirty-six verses), in which Jehovah speaks, announcing in solemn language the final doom of Israel's foes, and closing with a description of the glorious victory of the people of God. The first half of the book begins in gloom and closes in light; the second begins with judgment and ends with victory, the prophecy of the first part merging into apocalypse in the second. Really, but one great thought constitutes the prophet's entire message: one might label it *The Parable of Locusts,* and what it teaches. For the book of Joel is not made up, as so many other Old Testament books are, of the scattered "notes" of a long prophetic ministry extending over several years, but is rather occupied with a description of a single incident with its moral and spiritual application.

III. *The Occasion.*—Joel obviously took as his text a plague of ordinary locusts, which for some time, apparently, had been causing national panic, and he describes their ravages as without a parallel in the history of the land. He says in 1 : 14 :

> What the *gazam* left, the *arbeh* has eaten;
> What the *arbeh* left, the *yelek* has eaten;
> What the *yelek* left, the *hasil* has eaten.

Or, as Haupt translates this verse :

> What the (old) locust left, the (newly hatched) hopper ate;
> What the hopper left, the (pupa) crawler ate;
> What the crawler left, the (mature) flier ate.

Thus, from the four synonyms employed by the prophet, it is apparent that four successive swarms are described, or, as Credner prefers, the several successive stages of the same swarm : for example, first the larva stage, then as grasshoppers, and finally as matured, flying locusts. In 2 :25 they are all mentioned a second time, the same names being used, but not in exactly the same order. From this latter passage it may be further inferred that the plague extended over a considerable period of time : "I will restore to you the years that the locust hath eaten." Yet, the usual length of a locust visitation seldom exceeds five months (cf. Rev. 9 :10).

To the ancient Hebrews the very name "locusts" seems to have suggested all that our English term "harpies" conveys—all that is woeful (cf. Deut. 28:38-42). Their scientific name is *Acridium peregrinum*. When first hatched they are quite black and resemble large ants, having no sign of wings; but as they develop they cast off their outer skins which become outgrown, and molt through three stages which are plainly distinguishable, namely, the larva or wingless stage, called by the Arabs *debbi;* the pupa, with wing sacks developing, called *gowga;* and the full-fledged flying locust, known as *jared.* The males are by far the handsomer, having a vivid yellow body; the females are larger, being a deep brown. The latter deposit their eggs four inches deep in the soil, no matter how hard. When the insects are fully developed they are about two and one-half inches long, their heads resembling horses; hence, called by the Germans *Heupferde,* "hay-horses"; by the Italians, *Cavaletta,* "little ponies"; by the Arabs, *Djesh Allah,* "God's army" (Joel 2: 25). And in fact they do resemble flying fighters, and they do climb over walls and enter homes, and make the air to quiver (2:7-10); they have been estimated to fly at the rate of twelve miles an hour.

IV. *Jerusalem's Locust Plague in 1915.*—A most vivid description of it by John D. Whiting appeared in the *National Geographic Magazine* for December, 1915. Mr. Whiting describes the plague as beginning late in February of that year, and as extending over all Palestine and Syria from the borders of Egypt to the Taurus mountains. Similar plagues are known to have overtaken at least portions of Palestine in the years 1845, 1865 (a year still remembered by the Arabs as *Sinet el-Jared,* "the year of the locusts"), 1892, 1899 and 1904. The following are some of the accompanying phenomena in 1915. A loud noise was heard before the locusts were seen, produced by the flapping of myriads of locust wings and resembling the distant rumbling of waves (cf. Rev. 9:9). The sun was suddenly darkened. Showers of their excrements fell thick and fast, resembling those of mice. Their elevation above the earth was at times hundreds of feet; at other times they flew quite low, detached numbers alighting. "In Jerusalem, at least," Mr. Whiting says, "they invariably came from the northeast, going towards the southwest, establishing the accuracy of Joel's account in chap. 2:20." Tons were captured and buried alive; many were thrown into cisterns, or into the Mediterranean Sea, and, when washed ashore, were collected and dried and used for fuel in Turkish baths. The government issued a proclamation in April, 1915, requiring every man from sixteen to sixty years of age to gather eleven pounds of locust eggs, daily, and deliver them to the officials. The stork, which the Arabs call *Abu Saad,* "the father of good luck," was especially numerous over Palestine in 1915, and greedily devoured the innumerable host of the locust-pest. Hens gorged themselves on them.

Mr. Aaronsohn, another witness of the plague in 1915, testifies that in less than two months after their first appearance, not only was every green leaf devoured, but the very bark was peeled from the trees, which stood out white and lifeless, like skeletons. The fields, he says, were stripped to the ground. Even Arab babies left by their mothers in the shade of some tree, had their faces devoured before their screams were heard. The natives accepted of the plague as a just judgment upon them because of their wickedness.

It was, accordingly, a calamity such as this, which Joel employed to call the husbandmen, the vine-dressers, the priests, and the drunkards of his day to repentance. In his picture of their ravages he describes the beasts and lower animals as also suffering with men, and as standing pathetic in their mute appeal—the dire calamity and their sufferings being an omen of the dread "day of Jehovah" which was about to come!

V. *Interpretation of the Locusts.*—The question arises: Shall we interpret Joel's locusts literally as a real locust plague of the prophet's time, or shall we treat them allegorically, and as future, pointing metaphorically to the four monarchies inimical to the kingdom of God as described in the Book of Daniel, namely the Babylonians, Persians, Greeks and Romans? Jewish Rabbis and the early Church Fathers inclined to allegorize these prophecies, the latter explaining, for example, "the wheat, the new wine, and the oil" of 2:24, as having been fulfilled in the church; the wheat pointing to the body of Christ, the new wine, to his blood, and the oil to the Holy Spirit! All such exegesis is of course unwarranted. Equally unconvincing is the interpretation of those who regard the locusts of Joel as real locusts but not as the *Orthoptera* of the desert, but rather as apocalyptic locust-warriors, belonging to the wonders of the end-time and crowding the atmosphere of the terrible "day of Jehovah." Gaebelein, for example, interprets the locusts of chap. 1 as

typical of what will take place during the times of
the Gentiles from Nebuchadnezzar onward (Dan.
2:36ff.), while those of chapter 2, he fancies, describe what will take place during the last part of
Daniel's "seventieth week," preceding the glorious
manifestation of the Lord (Dan. 9:27)! Such
chronological precision would be wonderful if it
were only intended. Merx's theory is the revival of
the old allegorico-typical interpretation. To him
the book of Joel is a sort of apocalyptic typology,
having no reference in it whatever to the prophet's
own present; for, not having been delivered orally,
as he assumes, it was never intended as anything else
but a purely apocalyptic or eschatological work.

But by far the best interpretation is the historical,
or literal; according to which these prophecies, like
those of most other prophetical books, spring out
of the circumstances of the prophet's own time. To
cut off all occasion for them makes Joel's work a
merely learned essay, or *Midrash,* on preceding
prophetic literature. How absurd to think that the
prophet is addressing a mythical audience when he
solemnly asks the elders, "Hath this been in your
days?" (1:2); or, when he rebukes the priests, saying, "Gird yourselves with sackcloth, and lament,
ye priests" (1:13, 14); or, when he again solemnly
exhorts the people, "Turn ye unto me . . . and
rend your heart and not your garments" (2:12,
13). It is certainly more reasonable to think that
the prophet was here speaking to real people, than
to suppose he was shooting at random in the air, or
addressing some far-away future generation! Furthermore, it is manifestly improbable that the
prophet would describe an army of real soldiers as

"*like* soldiers," or speak of real horsemen "*as* horse-men" (2:4-9). Hence, we may conclude that he must be speaking of real warriors under the figure of real locusts. The only really valid objection to this interpretation is the implication in 2:20, that they are described as coming from the *north;* but as we have already seen, the locusts that visited Jerusalem in 1915 came from that direction; there are other witnesses on record to the same effect.

VI. *Joel's Originality.*—Of Jesus it was said, "Never man so spake" (John 7:46); and yet Jesus did not invent the alphabet or create the Aramaic language. At best there is very little originality in the world; it is a question even as to what consti-tutes originality. It is certainly not saying a thing necessarily first; but rather, saying it best, and with an accent of authority. Now, Joel is original in exactly this sense. He has a distinct individuality. Elmslie says of him, "He is either the original pro-phetic quarry, or the latest conglomerate." But ir-respective of the prophet's date, all must admit that both his thoughts and his language, even though borrowed, passed through his own mind and issued from it bearing the stamp of his own individuality. Moreover, it is recognized that he must have been read by many prophets, for either he quotes nearly everything he says, or he was quoted by Amos, Isaiah, Micah, Nahum, Zephaniah, Obadiah, Eze-kiel, Malachi; and also by some of the psalmists. Reuss regarded his quoting so many as improbable. And, indeed, the general impression from reading Joel's book is that of smoothness and sequence of thought rather than of slavish reproduction. If Joel is early, then his religious thoughts may be regarded as a kind of prophetic chart which subsequent writers followed. The following considerations are in favor of Joel's originality.

1. *The day of Jehovah.*—Joel must have coined this expression, for, he leaves it at the point where Amos and later prophets take it up. Though an eschatological phrase, and therefore presumably late, it is imbedded in Old Testament prophecy from its earliest stage (cf. Amos 5:18; Isa. 2:12). Joel is probably the inventor of the conception. For, the idea of a great Judgment Day comes forth from his hand so perfect, that his successors have adopted it and been able to add to it hardly a single touch. It was the visitation of a plague of locusts which, first, suggested it to Joel's mind.

2. *Literary independence.*—Two examples will be sufficient to demonstrate the claim: (a) The thought in 3:16, "And Jehovah will roar from Zion, and utter his voice from Jerusalem; and the heavens and the earth shall shake; but Jehovah will be a refuge unto his people, and a stronghold to the children of Israel" is obviously prior to Amos 1:2, which reads, "And he said, Jehovah will roar from Zion, and utter his voice from Jerusalem; and the pastures of the shepherds shall mourn, and the top of Carmel shall wither." For, in Joel it is the climax of a revelation; whereas Amos starts out with it, taking it, as it were, for his text. (b) In Joel 3:10, Jehovah exhorts the heathen, "Beat your plowshares into swords"; whereas, in Isa. 2:4 and in Mic. 4:3, these later prophets predict a time when the men of Judah "shall beat their swords into plowshares." The actual naturally precedes the ideal!

3. *The outpouring of the Spirit.*—Joel foretells

more explicitly than any other the outpouring of the Spirit upon all flesh (2:28, 29). This prediction has entitled him to be called, as he often is, "the prophet of Pentecost." And yet, Joel probably had but a vague appreciation of what these words really meant in the great program of God. To him they probably conveyed no more than a clearer perception of truth through dream and vision—a fulfilment of Moses' wish, "Would that all Jehovah's people were prophets, that Jehovah would put his Spirit upon them" (cf. Num. 11:29); for, "thoughts beyond their thoughts to those high bards were given." Hence, Joel himself was not so profoundly spiritual. For example, he does not begin to rise to Hosea's heights of Jehovah's lovingkindness, nor to Isaiah's transcendent pinnacles of Jehovah's holiness. On the other hand, he couples with the gift of the Spirit outward material blessings such as the former and the latter rains, new wine and oil, plenty and satisfaction (2:23-26), and treats them as related to each other almost as cause and effect; the material preceding the spiritual. There is, accordingly, a primitive originality about this feature of his prophecies, which justifies the spelling of the word "spirit" in this passage with a small letter, as it actually is in the English Revised Version. Besides, the restricted offer of salvation in verse 32 is a further hint of the prophet's primitive originality.

VII. *Date.*—Franz Delitzsch, forty years ago, confidently alleged that the great antiquity of the prophet Joel is a "certainty." On the contrary, some twenty years ago, Cornill quite as boldly affirmed, "Few results of Old Testament research are as surely determined and as firmly established as

that the Book of Joel dates from the century between Ezra and Alexander the Great." Calvin
more cautiously left the matter an open question:
"Quia nihil certi constat satius est tempus quo
docuit in medio relinquere." The most recent critical opinion assigns it to the generation following the
Maccabean age. But the apocalyptic character of
the book, in and of itself, should place the student
on his guard not to be too dogmatic; for no one can
actually guess when God *must* unveil himself in
revelation or apocalypse!

There is one fact, however, which more than any,
or all others together, helps to determine the date
of the book, namely, its place among the Twelve.
Both in the Hebrew Canon and in the Septuagint,
Joel is grouped among the early, pre-exilic prophets;
thus, in the Hebrew Canon, the order is Hosea, Joel,
Amos, Obadiah, Jonah, Micah, etc.; that of the
Septuagint, Hosea, Amos, Micah, Joel, Obadiah,
Jonah, etc. Very obviously, therefore, the rabbis
of antiquity regarded Joel as one of the earlier prophets. This fact creates at once a strong presump-
tion in favor of its early date. On the other hand,
if the book were written late, near the time when
the canonization of the prophets took place, it would
seem strange that the framers of the Canon should
have deemed him early!

Internal evidence, however, is worthy of examination and consideration; and on the whole, it argues
for an early origin:

1. No king is mentioned by Joel; but neither do
Nahum, Micah, or Habakkuk.

2. No idols are mentioned, and there is no allusion to the northern kingdom of Israel; but Joel

preached to Judah and Jerusalem where there was at least nominal worship of Jehovah.

3. No mention of Assyria; neither is there any in Amos.

4. "Elders" are spoken of as though they constituted the technical governing class of the age; as "Sheikhs" in later times (Joel 1:2, 14; 2:16); on the contrary, they stand as the experienced citizens of the community, not as state officials, and in 2:16 are set over against children and sucklings.

5. The prophet shows great devotion to sacrifices and ritual; but 2:13 is absolutely free of all ritual. In fact, no other prophet presents religion with less ritual.

6. No prophetic denunciations; but post-exilic prophets such as Haggai and Malachi did rebuke particular sins.

7. The "Grecians" are mentioned as active agents in the slave trade of the prophet's day (3:6); but Amos also complains of the slave trade in his time (Amos 1:6-9), and we know from archæology that the Grecians are mentioned both by Sargon II, 722-705 B. C., and in the Tell el-Amarna tablets of the fourteenth century B. C.

8. Philistines are mentioned (3:4); but the Philistines are little heard of after the Exile.

9. Edom and Egypt, also, are named (3:19); but Edom is known to have revolted under Jehoram in the ninth century B. C. (II Kings 8:20-22), and Shishak of Egypt invaded Judah in the time of Rehoboam (I Kings 14:25-28).

10. Jerusalem is described as having been plundered (3:17); Shishak is said to have done so (I Kings 14:26).

11. The people are described as "scattered" (3: 2) and as a reproach among the nations (2:19); but the language does not require us to think of the downfall of Jerusalem in 586 B. C.

12. Jehovah promises to "bring back the captivity" of Judah and Jerusalem (3:1, 4); but Hosea and Amos, when allowed to speak for themselves, hold out the same hope to Israel, and in the same language (Hos. 6:11; Amos 9:14).

13. Joel speaks of a "remnant" (2:32); but Isaiah uses the same identical word (Isa. 1:9). Besides, this concept, enshrined in different synonyms, is predominatingly employed by the prophets long before the exile.

14. Finally, Joel either borrows from others, or they from him. It is estimated that twenty-seven phrases, clauses, or expressions in the seventy-three verses of Joel's book have parallels in other Old Testament writings. But Joel 2:2 is clearly quoted in Zeph. 1:15, the phrases, "a day of darkness and gloominess, a day of clouds and thick darkness," being common to both; for in Joel they are an integral part of his picture of the approaching locusts, whereas, in Zephaniah they are more rhetorical embellishments, re-enforcing the prophet's accumulated description of the "day of Jehovah."

Now, most of these data are obviously too indefinite to be of any very great value in deciding the prophet's date, the records of no one period completely accounting for every reference in the book. Hence, it becomes necessary to fall back on the prophet's position in the order of the Twelve, and upon the fact of his originality which is so pronounced; and, accordingly, we are forced to conclude that Joel flourished early in the history of the divided kingdom, perhaps as early as the closing years of the ninth century B. C. For this conclusion there may be insufficient proof, but it is far more convincing than the purely arbitrary reasoning of McFadyen, who says, "The question is much more than an academic one, for on the answer to it will depend our whole conception of the development of Hebrew prophecy. . . . It is customary to deny to the pre-exilic prophets any word of promise or consolation to their own people!" The question, however, is not so easily settled. Credner in 1831 argued for its pre-exilic origin; Vatke, about the same time, was the first to make it post-exilic; while recently Haupt and Sellers, following Michaelis (1782), and Jahn (who, though he allowed Joel wrote in 690 B. C., claimed his prophecies referred to the Maccabean Age), bring it down to 140-130 B. C.

VIII. *Style*.—"Joel's style is in striking contrast," says G. B. Gray, "to the dull——not to say stilted—style of Haggai and the semi-rabbinic periods of Malachi." Bewer confirms this judgment and gives as his estimate of Joel's style, clearness, fluency, and beauty; adding that "as a lyrical poet he stands among the best of the Old Testament, being graphic, terse, and exceedingly effective." Joel resembles Amos, who, though one of the earliest of all the prophets, was the author of the purest and most classical Hebrew in the Bible. Ewald relied upon the purity of Joel's style as evidence of his antiquity. Early Hebrew literature is characterized by rhythm, just such as Joel displays. The ravages of the locusts are described in an expressive rhythmic staccato movement of poetic imagery, by which he pictures the rapid advance of the pest and their irresistible attack upon the city. In general, "His poetry," as Wünsche observes, "is distinguished by the soaring flight of imagination, and by the originality, beauty, and variety of his images and similes." In all these particulars Joel is surpassed by few. He even shows skill in the use of parallelism (1:10), and hyperbole (2:30, 31); and deigns like Isaiah, to employ paronomasia, or play on words, to make his pictures graphic and more vivid (1:12, 15; 3:12).

IX. *The Religious Teaching of Joel.*—1. The fundamental teaching of permanent religious value in the book of Joel is the prophet's clear, definite, and as we think, original, conception of the *Day of Jehovah.* This phrase occurs in the book five times (1:15; 2:1, 11, 31; 3:14), and signifies as Davidson has well put it, "the moment when Jehovah grasps the reins, which he seems to have held slackly before, when the currents of his moral rule, which had been running sluggishly, receive a mysterious quickening, and the Lord's work upon the earth is at last fully performed."

Or, as Gaebelein expresses it, it means "the day on which Jehovah will manifest himself as God;" the ultimate day of Jehovah; a day of both terror and blessing; a day of vengeance and the year of the redeemed; the day on which the eternal principles of Divine righteousness and human duty will be demonstrated; the final day of reckoning. Joel announced this "day" to Judah; Amos, later on, announced it to Israel (Amos 1:2; 6:3; 9:11-15). This is the principal teaching of Joel.

2. Out of this first great teaching grew others of

a practical character, one of which was *repentance* (2:12-17). Joel exhorts his readers to repentance, promising that by it they may avert the day of terror. They respond to his exhortation and the plague of locusts is removed; and material and spiritual blessings follow (2:18-32). This urgent summons of the prophet to repentance has been adopted by the Anglican Church for the first solemn day of Lent.

3. The other great teaching of the book is the *outpouring of the Spirit upon all flesh* (2:28, 29). This, on the one hand, was a fulfilment of Num. 11:29; and, on the other it was fulfilled on the Day of Pentecost (Acts 2:16 ff.); "fulfilled," indeed, but not exhausted! It is a promise which was destined to receive a repeated and ever-increasing fulfilment. Peter in pointing to this prediction of Joel on that memorable occasion, did not omit its terror. Grace and judgment always move side by side. The fall of Jerusalem was the sequel of the Day of Pentecost. The whole thought is pre-eminently eschatological; yet it was meant primarily for the comfort of the people in the prophet's own time. It is akin to Jeremiah's promise of a "new covenant" (Jer. 31:31-34). Though there is no prediction of the Messiah in the book of Joel, yet as Horton well observes, "Our study of the book should lead us to Christ and the baptism of the Spirit." Thus Joel begins to bridge the chasm to the kingdom of grace.

SPECIAL LITERATURE ON JOEL

A. B. Davidson, "The Prophet Joel," *Expositor* (1888); G. B. Gray, "The Parallel Passages in Joel in their bearing on the question of date," *Expositor*

(1893); W. L. Pearson, *The Prophecy of Joel* (Dissertation, 1885); O. R. Sellers, *The Book of Joel* (A Thesis, based on Prof. Haupt's Lectures; read in Ms. 1922); A. C. Gaebelein, *The Prophet Joel* (1909); K. A. Credner, *Der Prophet Joel, übersetzt und erklärt* (1831); A. Wünsche, *Die Weissagung des Propheten Joel übersetzt und erklärt* (1872); A. Merx, *Die Prophetie des Joel und ihre Ausleger* (1879); A. Scholz (R. C.), *Kommentar zum Buche des Propheten Joel* (1885); H. Holzinger, "Sprachcharakter und Abfassungszeit des Buches Joel." *ZATW* (1889); Eugène la Savoureux, *Le prophète Joel* (1888); G. Preuss, *Die Prophetie Joels mit besonderen Beruchsichtigung der Zeitfrage* (1891); Graetz, *Der einheitliche Character der Prophetie Joels* (1873); S. Oettli, *Der Prophet Joel* (Vortrag, 1888); G. Kessner, *Das Zeitalter des Propheten Joel* (1888); Knieschke, *Die Eschatologie des Buches Joel in ihrer historisch-geographischen Bestimmtheit* (1912).

CHAPTER III

AMOS THE PROPHET OF JUSTICE

I. *The Man.*—By many Amos is supposed to be
the earliest prophet whose writings have come down
to us. If so, then his book is the oldest volume of
"sermons" extant! Be that as it may, he is one of
the most forceful preachers of repentance and judgment of all the prophets of the Old Testament.
As Cornill keenly observes, "Amos is one of the
most wonderful appearances in the history of the
human spirit." His name, however, which signifies
"burden" or "burden-bearer," should be carefully
distinguished from "Amoz," the father of Isaiah, as
the spelling in Hebrew differs. Like Elijah, and
Luther, and other religious reformers, he was both
the product and representative of his age. Stern,
fearless, self-contained, a man of granite-make, he
possessed a powerful well-knit mind and a vivid
imagination, and is one of the most arresting figures
ever on the stage of Hebrew history. He was not
only the first of the prophets who wrote down what
he preached, but the pioneer of a new era.

II. *His Home and Early Occupation.*—Reared
on the edge of the desert, twelve miles south of
Jerusalem "among the herdsmen of Tekoa" (1:1),
he was a rustic, like Micah; and, because his father's
name is nowhere mentioned, it is inferred that he

probably sprang from a poor and obscure family.
He was a shepherd, and, therefore, a natural-born
preacher! He raised a peculiar breed of stunted,
fine-wooled sheep (as the Hebrew word, *noked,* in
1:1, when assisted by the Arabic cognate, implies),
a breed small in size, and ugly in appearance, but
highly esteemed on account of their wool; and he describes himself as also "a dresser of sycamore trees"
(7:14). Thus, he lived close to nature. In the
desolate districts of Judah sloping rapidly toward
the Dead Sea eastward, where wild beasts often
lurked, doubtless he had often studied the stars, observed the moon's changing phases, and marvelled
at the full-orbed sun as it rose over the distant
ranges of Moab. Constantly breathing the keen
fresh air of the desert, and often climbing to the
peaks of the loftiest heights, he lived, as G. A. Smith
expresses it, "in the face of wide horizons, the land-
scape of the desert becoming sacraments of the divine
presence." His occupation naturally carried him to
the wool markets of the northern cities. There he
would become acquainted with the life and religion
of the people. Though he was untutored, having
lived as a shepherd in the isolated and desert regions
of Tekoa, yet being by birth a morally noble, healthy
and vigorous yeoman, like John the Baptist who
spent most of his years in the same wilderness, he
developed into a religious reformer, and, eventually,
became supremely concerned for the rights of God,
and for justice.

III. *His Call to Preach.*—Amos had no special,
professional, or formal preparation to preach; he
was educated rather in the school of vigilance. By
inheritance he was neither a prophet nor a prophet's

son; that is, he belonged to no established guild,
such as "the sons of the prophets." On the contrary, Jehovah took him, he says, "from following
the flock," and said unto him, "Go prophesy unto
my people Israel" (7:14, 15). There, in the lonely
wilderness, perhaps "under the terror of a storm,"
as Bertholet suggests, the shadow fell upon his soul
which made him aware of God's coming judgments,
and forced him to lift up his voice in lamentation
over his people (5:1). Such rustics when called
from the open life of the country to the feverish atmosphere of the city, become often experts in society,
bringing with them "facts into politics and vision
into religion." His mission was particularly to
North Israel. Accordingly, he repaired to Bethel,
twelve miles north of Jerusalem, and there under the
very shadow of the royal palace lifted up his voice
in a vigorous and impassioned cry for justice.

IV. *His Period.*—The title to his prophecies de-
fines his period as "in the days of Uzziah king of
Judah, and in the days of Jeroboam the son of
Joash king of Israel, two years before the earthquake" (1:1). These statements are in general amply confirmed by the contents of the prophecy (6:
13; 7:11). The date of the earthquake, however, is
somewhat uncertain. But it must have been one of
unusual severity, as it is alluded to by Zechariah,
who preached more than two hundred years later
(Zech. 14:5). A total eclipse of the sun seems to
have accompanied it (supposed to be referred to in
8:9), which astronomers have calculated as having
taken place June 15, 763 B. C. This would fix the
prophet's date as somewhere about 760 B. C. This
was the golden age of North Israel, the high water

mark of their national prosperity. Jeroboam II was then upon the throne. He was a strong king. He ruled over a very large extent of territory, as Jonah had predicted he would (II Kings 14:25). But unfortunately, though there was much wealth in the nation, there was little wisdom. Feasting and banquets took the place of religious endeavor. A spirit of greed ruled society. Corruption of justice was a common sin. Might became right. Land seizure was an everyday crime. The landlords had all the legal machinery at their command to oppress. The result was that the rich became richer and the poor became poorer. With scornful indifference men lived "at ease in Zion" (6:1). Love of luxury prevailed, as prior to the downfall of Rome, and the breaking out of the French Revolution. Religion lost all its vitality, and morals were completely ignored. Insincerity and dishonesty, corruption and licentiousness, criminal extravagance and blind assurance took such a firm hold of the wealthy, arrogant voluptuaries, that they became heathen in everything but name. No wonder that the prophet of the wilderness was shocked beyond endurance and that he indignantly pronounces doom upon the nation. The only surprise is that he did not condemn the calves at Bethel and at Dan, and announce by name the agent of their destruction. Strange, he never mentions Assyria!

V. *His Literary Style.*—Though one of the earliest, perhaps the first of the writing prophets, as we have seen, there is nothing crude, unfinished, or unrefined about his style. On the contrary he is the author of the purest and most classical Hebrew in the entire Old Testament. Jerome describes him

as *imperitus sermone, sed non scientia,* "rude in
speech but not in knowledge"; but, among the Hebrews, the best writing is an unaffected transcript
of the best speaking. And so it ought to be always
and everywhere. Jewish tradition accused him of
having had an impediment in his speech, but such a
tradition is not justified by the prophet's speech.
Amos was an orator. His style is grave, measured,
and rhetorical. He uses brief uninvolved sentences,
and often indulges in questions, apostrophes, and
exclamations; he understands the power of repeti-
tion, and has enriched his message with varied imagery, and bucolic figures derived from nature, of
which perforce he was an ardent and constant student. For example, he exhorts Israel to "seek him
that maketh the Pleiades and Orion," (5:8), and ad-
monishes them that they shall be rescued from the
enemy "as a shepherd rescueth out of the mouth of
the lion two legs, or a piece of an ear" (3:12). And
he constantly employs as metaphors and symbols the
implements of rural life, such as threshing instruments (1:13), harvest carts (2:13), plowing and
oxen (6:12), baskets of summer fruit (8:1), sieves
(9:9), the gin and the snare (3:5), fishhooks (4:
2); and he, also, speaks of plowmen and reapers, of
sowers and grape-treaders (9:13), of gardens and
vineyards (4:9), of locusts and earthquakes (1:1;
7:1; 8:8; 9:5); so that his vocabulary and style are
conspicuously those of Oriental homeliness, and especially of the wilderness. His sentences are regular,
well-balanced and flowing, even rising at times to
lyrical outbursts of poetic delineation; they are characterized by even paranomasia and rhythm. Quite
possibly, after he had preached at Bethel, he re-

turned to Tekoa, and wrote down his prophecies in a book.

VI. *The Essence of his Message.*—Samaria delenda est, "Samaria must be destroyed!" This is the essence of his book. The nation is ripe for judgment. Amos is the first of the prophets to declare the doom of North Israel. On a high feast day at Bethel he opened his lamentation, crying, "The virgin of Israel is fallen; she shall no more rise" (5:2). That was the funeral dirge of the nation! Serious and grave indeed was the situation. The day of Israel's doom was come: the Day of Jehovah! He took up this idea where Joel had left off: beginning, "Jehovah will roar from Zion and utter his voice from Jerusalem" (1:2). It was a day of national revelation! With unparalleled audacity, Amos announced to the people, lulled and dulled with prosperity, the results which must inevitably follow when religion is divorced from morality; enunciating with greatest emphasis and unprecedented clarity the doctrine, "Nothing can be good in Him, which evil is in me!" The causes for such judgment were patent: wealth and luxury, frivolity and corruption, opulence and oppression, summer and winter palaces, ivory couches, songs of revelry and wine,—these were enough to convince the clear-headed prophet of the desert that there was left but one course for Providence; besides, there were specific crimes still more culpable and worthy of censure: namely, victimizing the poor, confiscating their garments for debt, unbridled licentiousness even under the cloak of religion, hypocritical tithing, and hollow Sabbath-observance, even pilgrimages to far distant shrines,—these and other evils made the sensitive soul of Amos so to burn with indignation that he could not do otherwise than lift up his voice in protestation. He discovered moral unsoundness everywhere, and he was clearly and overwhelmingly convinced that Jehovah had appointed him the *corrector morum* of his age. His message, therefore, was a gospel, but it was the gospel of law and not of grace!

VII. *The Analysis and Contents of His Book.*— His prophecies fall naturally into three divisions:

A. Chapters 1-2, a series of eight formal judgments on Israel and their neighbors: thus, eight times over expressed, "For three transgressions and for four I will not turn away the punishment of,

1. *Damascus,* for threshing Gilead, (1:3-5);

2. Gaza, for delivering captives to Edom (1:6-8);

3. *Tyre,* also, for delivering captives to Edom (1:9-10);

4. *Edom,* for pursuing his brother without pity (1:11-12);

5. *Ammon,* for cruelty to Gilead (1:13-15);

6. *Moab,* for burning the bones of the king of Edom to lime (2:1-3);

7. Judah, for rejecting the law of Jehovah (2:4-5); and

8. *Israel,* for selling "the righteous for silver and the needy for a pair of shoes" (2:6-16), the whole series teaching the fundamental principles of Biblical sociology, namely, (1) the universal sovereignty of God; (2) the sin of inhumanity; and (3) the moral responsibility of all mankind. Amos was the first prophet of the Hebrews to preach internationalism; that there is such a thing as international morality!

B. Chapters 3-6, three discourses of threatening and doom, each one beginning with the exhortation, "Hear ye this word" (3:1; 4:1; 5:1), all three strongly minatory:

1. Jehovah's choice of Israel conditional (chap. 3),—the greatest chapter in the book!

2. A warning to the Ladies of Samaria, who are inexcusably thoughtless, selfish, and cruel (chap. 4; cf. Isa. 3:16 ff.); for, in spite of repeated admonitions: (a) famine (vs. 6); (b) drought (vss. 7, 8); (c) blasting and mildew (vs. 9); (d) pestilence and sword (vs. 10); and (e) earthquake (vs. 11), they have not returned unto Jehovah. Therefore, shouts the prophet, "Prepare to meet thy God O Israel!" (vs. 12).

3. An elegy over the nation, whose recovery is impossible (chaps. 5-6); because (a) they spurn righteousness (5:7); (b) hate reproof (5:10); (c) court recklessly the day of reckoning (5:18); (d) reduce religion to formal ritual (5:21); and (e) scorn the divine entreaties "to seek Jehovah and live (5:4, 6, 14). Whereupon, the prophet pronounces a double woe upon Israel and their princes: "they shall go into captivity and their palaces shall be destroyed" (6:7, 8, 11).

C. Chapters 7-9. A series of five visions, interrupted by the priest of Bethel (7:10-17), and ending with an epilogue of hope and comfort (9:7-15):

1. A vision of locusts (7:1-3);

2. A vision of devouring fire (7:4-6);

3. A vision of the plumbline of rectitude (7:7-9). At this point Amaziah, the priest of Bethel, challenges the prophet's right to fulminate thus vehemently against the house of king Jeroboam;

whereupon, Amos boldly repudiates the priest's charge of prophesying for a living, and claims that his inspiration is independent of all artificial training in the schools; hence, he daringly defies both him and the king! (7:10-17). By this incident, one is reminded of John Knox, and the motto which is still to be found inscribed, close beneath the ceiling, on the four walls of his "study" in High Street, Edinburgh: it reads, "I am in the place where conscience bids me speak the truth, therefore, the truth I speak, impugn it who so list!"

4. A vision of a basket of summer fruit *(kăyitz)*; Jehovah responding, "The end *(kātz)* is come!" (8:1-14). Note the pun which Amos puts into Jehovah's mouth!

5. A vision of the smitten sanctuary (9:1-6); the people being pictured as buried under the ruins of their false religion.

The book concludes with a promise of restoration, —a paragraph of singular beauty, both hopeful and comforting, assuring Israel that the nation shall be sifted and a remnant ultimately restored (9:7-15).

VIII. *The Permanent Value of His Message to Us.*—In these brief sermons of the prophet may be found certain great fundamental truths of special eternal worth: for example,

1. Amos vindicates the moral personality of God, emphasizing that the essence of the divine nature is absolute righteousness. For a long time it has been the fashion to see in Amos the creator of ethical monotheism; but, as Sellin observes, "that is an error. He was only the deepest, the most uncompromising and most eloquent herald of a truth that had long been known." It was Amos' mission to

interpret Jehovah as a God of righteousness. He
does not attempt to give either a system of theology
or a treatise on moral philosophy, but he does seek
to awaken Israel's conscience by pointing to the
absolute righteousness of Jehovah. For, the God
of Amos is not only all-powerful and international,
he is also ethical and spiritual. The prophet's three
apostrophes to Jehovah are especially majestic and
noteworthy (4:13; 5:8; 9:5, 6).

2. Amos also taught that the most elaborate worship, if insincere, is but an insult to God: "I hate, I
despise, your feasts, and I will take no delight in
your solemn assemblies" (5:21); and, "Take thou
away from me the noise of thy songs; for I will not
hear the melody of thy viols" (5:23). Such words
are eloquent to generations far beyond the age in
which they were spoken. Many a modern Christian
seems to be unable to conceive of salvation apart
from the sacraments and ceremonies of his own
church. Amos taught Israel that religion means
much more than mere worship, and that it is not
the smoke of the burnt offering that is acceptable
to God, but the incense of a true and loyal heart.

3. And he further taught that there must be social
justice between man and man: "Let justice roll down
as waters, and righteousness as a mighty stream"
(5:24). The great mission of Amos was essentially
that of a reformer whose work is to sweep away
abuses, to overthrow established evils, and thus to
prepare for a reconstruction, which necessarily he
must leave to others. Of such the world has constant need. The great passion of the prophet's soul
was for social justice. To him this was a fundamental postulate of society. Hence, he urged the

inexorable character of the moral law (2:6-8). Morality was the one necessity of Israel. God's requirements are always moral. Moral issues determine the course of history. By such preaching Amos lighted a social candle in Israel that has never been, indeed, never can be, extinguished. His whole message serves as a most fitting prelude to James' definition of religion: "Pure religion and undefiled before our God and Father is this, to visit the fatherless and widows in their affliction, and to keep oneself unspotted from the world" (James 1:27).

4. Another great truth taught by Amos is the fact that privilege involves responsibility: "You only have I known of all the families of the earth; therefore, I will visit upon you all your iniquities (3:2). Election to privilege is consequently only another name for election to duty!

5. And another is the meaning and purpose of calamity: "I have given you want of bread, yet have ye not returned unto me, saith Jehovah" (4:6 ff.). Every disaster is but a new call to repentance (cf. Lk. 13:1-5).

6. And another, that warning is never obsolete. This great truth is taught practically throughout the entire book. There is a gospel in Amos, but it is "the gospel of the Lion's Roar!"

7. And, still another lesson is, The necessity of personal conviction in a prophet (7:14, 15). Religion is a personal matter; likewise conviction; it cannot be inherited!

8. Finally, the book of Amos has special historical value: being the oldest of the prophetic writings *which is undisputed,* it becomes an important witness to the religious beliefs current in Israel

during the eighth century B.C. Amos not only recognized the moral precepts of Jehovah as binding
upon Israel (5:21-27), but he judges Israel by a
broad moral standard which he regards as binding
upon all nations. It was by teachings such as these
that he influenced the prophets who succeeded him,
Isaiah, Micah, Jeremiah and Ezekiel.

IX. *Special Passages of Peculiar Interest:*—

1. "Shall two walk together except they have
agreed" (3:3)! This passage is especially Oriental.
As is well known, in the East it is dangerous to
travel through deep wadies and over rugged mountain roads, with unknown, untried, and possibly
inimical companions.

2. "Surely the Lord Jehovah will do nothing,
except he reveal his secret unto his servants the
prophets" (3:7). There is, accordingly, an esoteric
element in all true preaching. God whispers his
secrets to those who are willing to "speak for"
him!

3. "Did ye bring unto me sacrifices and offerings
in the wilderness forty years, O house of Israel?"
(5:25). The implication is that they did not; the
reason being that from the prophet's point of view,
"to obey is better than sacrifice" (cf. I Sam. 15:22).

4. "Woe to them that are at ease in Zion"
(6:1). Carlyle remarks that "Socrates was terribly
at ease"!

5. "That they may possess *(yĕrĕshu)* the remnant of Edom *(ĕdhōm)*, and all the nations that
are called by my name" (9:12). Through slight
changes, almost infinitesimal in the Hebrew, the
Septuagint translators (c. 250 B.C.) rendered this
passage: "That the residue of men *(âdhâm)* may

seek after *(yĭdrĕshu)* the Lord" (these last two words being supplied as a necessary object to the transitive verb "seek"); and so it is quoted by James at the Council in Jerusalem, A.D. 50 (Acts 15:17). This passage is especially interesting as an outstanding example in textual criticism.

6. "Behold the days come, saith Jehovah, that the plowman shall overtake the reaper, and the treader of grapes him that soweth seed" (9:13). In this one sentence Amos condenses the gist of his hope for the future; and though the picture is wholly materialistic, it is a classical expression of the Messianic kingdom, for which Israel longed, in all its outward glory and grandeur.

SPECIAL LITERATURE ON AMOS

J. E. McFadyen, "A Cry for Justice, A Study in Amos," *The Short Course Series* (1912); E. A. Edghill, "The Book of Amos," *Westminster Commentaries* (1914); A. B. Davidson, "The Prophet Amos," *Biblical and Literary Essays* (Posthumous, 1902); H. G. Mitchell, *Amos, an Essay in Exegesis* (1893); W. R. Smith, *Prophets of Israel,* Lecture III (1882); S. R. Driver, "Joel and Amos," *The Cambridge Bible,* (1897); also, articles on "Amos" in the various *Dictionaries of the Bible, Encyclopedias,* etc., and the numerous *Introductions to the Old Testament* (cited under Hosea); G. Baur, *Der Prophet Amos erklärt* (1847); J. H. Gunning, *De god-spraken van Amos* (1885); J. J. P. Valeton, *Amos en Hosea* (1894); the same translated into German (1898); Oettli, *Amos und Hosea* (1901); Löhr, "Unter suchungen zum Buch Amos," *Beihefte zur ZATW* (1901); Baumann, "Der Aufbau der Amosreden," *Beihefte zur ZATW* (1903); Sievers and Guthe, *Amos, metrisch bearbeitet* (1907); Winter, "Analyze des Buches Amos," *Theologische Studien und Kritiken* (1910); H. Schmidt, *Der Prophet Amos* (1917); Köhler, *Amos* (1917); K. Budde, "Zur Geschichte des Buches Amos," in the Wellhausen *Festschrift* (1914); K. Marti, "Zur Komposition von Amos, 1:3–2:3", in the Baudissin *Festschrift* (1918).

CHAPTER IV

OBADIAH THE CENSURER OF RIDICULE

I. *The Book.*—Obadiah is the shortest book in the Old Testament, having only twenty-one verses. It is never quoted or even echoed in the New Testament, unless perchance vs. 21 is reflected in Rev. 11:15. The book stands among the Twelve immediately after Amos. König and others account for its position here on the supposition that the framers of the Canon probably regarded Obadiah as in effect an expansion of the short prediction against Edom in Amos 9:12. The title describes it as a "vision" and as directed against Edom; George Adam Smith has dubbed it "an indignant oration." Though brief, it is difficult: its difficulty being, as Robertson Smith observes, "out of all proportion to its length."

II. *The Author.*—Obadiah is without any personal history; however, his name, which means "worshiper of Jehovah," is suggestive. He bore a very common name among the Semites, especially in post-exilic times; compare Abdiel, "servant of Jehovah," (I Chron. 5:15), and the Arabic name Abdallah, "servant of God." Attempts have been made to identify our prophet with some one of the dozen or more Obadiahs mentioned in the Old Testament, e.g.:

1. Obadiah, the steward in Ahab's palace who hid the Lord's prophets by fifty in a cave (I Kings 18:3-16).

2. Obadiah, the teacher of the law sent out by Jehoshaphat into the cities of Judah (II Chron. 17:7).

3. The "man of God" in Amaziah's time who advised the king not to allow the army of North Israel to accompany him against the Edomites (II Chron. 25:7).

4. Obadiah, one of the overseers, in repairing the temple under Josiah (II Chron. 34:12).

To our prophet, however, evidently his "work was more important than the worker; and for the sake of the work, the author himself allowed his personality to slip into the background!"

III. *The Message.*—Obadiah's entire message may be summed up in a couple of phrases: the destruction of Edom (vss. 1-16) and the restoration of Israel (vss. 17-21). The prophet directed his words, however, not so much as a warning to Edom as a message of comfort to Israel.

A threefold analysis of the book frequently given is the following:

1. Verses 1-9, the ruin of Edom, despite her being securely sheltered in rocky fastnesses.

2. Verses 10-14, the reasons for it; namely, her cruelty to Jacob and her rejoicing over Judah's adversity.

3. Verses 15-21, retribution to Edom and restoration to Israel.

Bewer's interpretation and chronological arrangement of the prophecy is typical of the modern school. He regards the book as composite and as the product of four different authors who lived at widely separated times, thus:

(a) First, there are imbedded in the book the prophecies of an ancient pre-exilic seer, who, hearing that certain nations were rallying to attack Edom and being persuaded that Jehovah was behind the movement, hoped they would succeed, and in fact predicted Edom's defeat (vss. 1-4).

(b) These words of this ancient prophet were in due time taken up by Obadiah, who probably lived about 450 B.C., when a great catastrophe befell Edom, through the invasion of the Nabatheans, or early Arabs, and seeing their fulfilment in the events which were then taking place about him, and recalling how the Edomites had rejoiced over the downfall of Jerusalem in 586 B.C., thrilled with emotion, he broke forth into passionate warnings, saying, "as thou hast done, so is it done to thee; thy dealing shall return upon thine own head" (vss. 5-14, 15b).

(c) Then, perhaps a hundred years later, when the Edomites were forced into the Negeb and Southern Judah, and had, accordingly, become nearer neighbors than ever to the Jews, continuing to hate each other, another unknown prophet of patriotic heart and patriotic mind lifted up his voice and declared that some day Jehovah would restore Israel to her former power and glory (vss. 15a, 16-18).

(d) Finally, in the period of the Maccabean uprising (B.C. 168 ff.), some one else added the conclusion to the book, in which he assured the Jews that Jehovah's kingdom would be established and that he, Jehovah, would reign alone (vss. 19-21).

Bewer's view is shared by others; but, there is slight ground for thinking that the prophet while predicting the future is really describing the past, or that "he speaks of what the Edomites had actually done as of what they ought not to do!"

IV. *Date.*—As the book is introduced by no historical or chronological data of any kind by which its age may be determined, we are thrown back on internal evidence. Accordingly, many widely divergent dates have been suggested, ranging from the time of Jehoram, king of Judah (ca. 850 B.C.), in whose reign the Philistines and Arabians attacked Jerusalem and carried away the possessions of the royal palace (II Chron. 21:16, 17), to 312 B.C. (a date suggested first by Hitzig), when the Nabatheans were in possession of Edom and Antigonus ordered an expedition sent against them.

Several factors enter into the decision of the question:

1. *Obadiah's place among the Twelve,* which in the Hebrew is fourth, the order being: Hosea, Joel, Amos, Obadiah, Jonah, Micah, etc.; in the Greek, however, fifth: Hosea, Amos, Micah, Joel, Obadiah, Jonah, etc., showing confessedly that the framers of the Canon (ca. 200 B.C.) regarded Obadiah as early.

2. *The unity of the book,* which is usually sacrificed by those who put Obadiah late. But, of course, the composite character of a book as short even as that of Obadiah is always possible. Modern hymns are not infrequently revised and emended, e. g., "I need thee every hour," and "God bless our native land."

3. *The vivid character of vss. 10-14,* which seem to describe as history the final overthrow of Jerusalem by Nebuchadnezzar in 586 B.C. Elmslie

argues: "It is not merely a disabled state, or a partially plundered capital that we have delineated here, but a dismembered and dispossessed and dispersed nation." Yet this is not by any means the unanimous judgment of all; Pusey, for example, makes these verses a *prediction*, not a *description*, of Jerusalem's downfall, while Davis finds an appropriate setting for them in Ahaz' reign, ca. 731 B.C., in whose time frequent calamities befell Judah, e.g.:

(1) Rezin, king of Damascus, wrested Elath from the Jews, drove them out, and let the Edomites dwell there (II Kings 16:6, in the LXX).

(2) Pekah, king of Israel, slew 120,000 of Judah and took 200,000 captives (II Chron. 28:6, 8).

(3) Zichri, a mighty man of Ephraim, slew the king's son (II Chron. 28:7).

(4) The Edomites smote Judah and carried away captives (II Chron. 28:17).

(5) The Philistines also invaded various cities of Judah (II Chron. 28:18).

(6) Ahaz even stripped the temple of its treasures in order to pay tribute to the king of Assyria (II Kings 16:8).

Surely such conditions explain reasonably well Obadiah's description of Jerusalem's calamity as one of "disaster," "distress," and "destruction" (vs. 12). Quite probably, then, the eighth century gave the prophecy birth.

Among those who favor an early date are Caspari, Delitzsch, Nägelsbach, Keil, v. Orelli, Kirkpatrick, Peters, and Pusey. On the other hand, those who argue for a late date, exilic or post-exilic, are Hitzig, Kuenen, Wellhausen, Nowack, Cornill, G. A. Smith, Elmslie, Bewer, Driver, and others.

V. *Edom.*—Obadiah prophesied, as we have seen, "concerning Edom," more particularly, concerning the inhabitants of Edom's rock citadel: "The pride of thy heart hath deceived thee, O thou that dwellest in the clefts of the rock *(Sela),* whose habitation is high" (vs. 3). The "rock" referred to here is almost certainly Petra, which doubtless from earliest times was the central stronghold of the nation. The modern Arabs call it *Wady Musa;* the ancient Syrians, as Josephus *(Antiq.* IV, vii, 1) tells us, called it "Rekem," after Rekem, the Midianite prince, who fell in battle with Israel in Moab in the days of Phinehas (Num. 31:8). For situation and natural beauty Petra is unique among the cities of earth. To describe it adequately is well-nigh an impossibility. Its location, deep down among the mountains of Seir, surrounded on all sides with richly colored rocks of simply matchless beauty and grandeur, renders it a "wonder of the desert." One enters the weird but attractive city enclosure by a narrow gorge, over a mile long, called the *Sik,* or cleft. This defile is one of the most magnificent and romantic avenues of its kind in all nature. A tiny stream flows under one's feet much of the way. The chasm is both narrow and deep, oftentimes so contracted as to be almost dark at noonday. The rocks which bound it are tinted most beautifully with all the colors of the rainbow. On emerging from it into the great hollow basin, (which is over a mile long by two-thirds of a mile broad), the explorer is confronted by rock-hewn dwellings, tombs, temples, and other cuttings on every side. Several hundreds of these, most of them doubtless mausolea originally, still remain, all carved literally out of the solid sandstone rock. The ruins of a castle and of buildings and the arches of a bridge, and columns, still stand scattered over the bottom of the city's site. The colors of the rocks add immensely to the attractiveness of the place. The deepest reds, purple, orange, yellow, white, violet, and other colors are arranged by nature in alternate bands, shading off artistically into one another, curving and twisting in gorgeous fantasies according to the infiltration of the oxides of iron, manganese, and other substances which so often produce in sandstone rocks color varieties of special beauty. The entire city and its environs are one immense maze of richly colored mountains and cliffs, chasms, rocky shelves and narrow valleys, gorges and plateaus, shady dells and sunny promontories, grand and beautiful; just the ideal of beauty and protection for a fortress of trade and commerce to satisfy an oriental nomad. But, alas! desolation now reigns within and about it on every hand, and Obadiah's warnings and predictions have been woefully verified!

VI. *Teachings.*—Such a brief book should not be expected to teach many great and valuable lessons. Three may be mentioned:

1. *The prophet's warning against ridicule* (vs. 12).—Ridicule springs from pride. When we ridicule others we reveal the spirit in ourselves. To ridicule betrays a lack of brotherly love. It is often an evidence of real hate. Edom and Israel scorned and hated each other throughout their whole history. For centuries there existed between them an implacable animosity. They constantly waged a war of revenge against each other. To a large degree it

was the result of selfish patriotism and tribal
jealousy.   Patriotism to many means little more
than national selfishness.   It easily degenerates into
pure arrogancy.   According to Tolstoi, "patriotism
is a vice and belongs to the tribal period."

2. *His doctrine of strict retribution* (vss. 10, 15).
—Obadiah taught with special emphasis the inde-
structible character of eternal justice.   A "day of Jehovah," he declared, is coming upon Edom and also
upon the nations.   Edom's vaunted wisdom will
completely fail her; her wise men will be blinded,—
for their own destruction.   Jehovah will take away
all wisdom from Edom so that none may escape
destruction (vss. 8, 9).   Edom "shall be cut off forever"; indeed, "the day of Jehovah is near upon all
nations" (vss. 10, 15).

3. *His sure hope of Israel's coming Golden Age.*
—"The house of Jacob shall possess their possessions" (vs. 17).   The Hebrew word here for "possessions," is a rare expression, and includes religious
possessions.   To the Christian, religious "possessions" mean far more; for, "the channels of grace
deepen as they run through scripture."

Finally, "saviours shall come up on mount Zion
to judge the mount of Esau; and the kingdom shall
be Jehovah's (vs. 21).   Edom subdued shall be
Edom incorporated.   This promise constitutes the
bright side of "the day of Jehovah."   It points to
the consummation of all human history.   The
prophet here expands his original predictions of
catastrophe on Edom to include, eschatologically, "a
world-judgment on all the heathen and the conse-
quent restoration of Israel.   It is the final word, not
only of Obadiah, but of all prophecy—a glimpse

really of the messianic kingdom for which all the prophets longed, and an interpretation of the self-consciousness of Israel. To-day the prophet's words are finding their slow but silent fulfilment in the sure advent of the kingdom of God and his Christ."

SPECIAL LITERATURE ON OBADIAH

1. *Commentaries, etc.*—Caspari, *Der Prophet Obadja* (1842); Perowne, "Obadiah and Jonah," *Cambridge Bible* (1889); Peters, *Die Prophetie Obadjahs* (1892); Douglas, "Obadiah and Zephaniah," *Handbooks for Bible Classes;* Delitzsch, art. "Wann weissagte Obadya?" in *Rudeb. u. Guer. Zeitschrift* (1851); Cheyne, art., "Obadiah," *Encyclopedia Biblica* (1902); Peckham, *Introduction to the Study of Obadiah* (1910); J. M. P. Smith, art., "The Structure of Obadiah," *American Journal of Semitic Languages and Literature* (1906).

2. *On Edom and Petra.*—Buhl, *Die Geschichte der Edomiter* (1893); Torrey, "The Edomites in Southern Judah," *Journal of Biblical Literature and Exegesis* (1898); Vincent, "Les Nabatheans," *Revue Biblique* (1898); Nöldeke, art. "Edom," *Encyclopedia Biblica,* (1910); Brünnow u. v., Domaszewski, *Die Provincia Arabia* (1904-9); Musil, *Arabia Petraea* (1908); Dalman, *Petra und seine Felsheiligtümer,* (1908); G. A. Smith, art., "The Land of Edom," *Expositor* (1908); Libbey and Hoskins, *The Jordan Valley and Petra* (1905).

CHAPTER V

JONAH THE PROPHET OF CATHOLICITY

The Book of Jonah is very largely biographical; there being, apart from his prayer in chapter 2, only one sentence which can in strictness be called prophetic discourse, 3:4. The personal experiences of other prophets, however, are also sometimes recorded in their books, cf. Hos. 1-3; Amos 7:10-15; Jer. 1, 25-29; 36-38.

I. *The Man and His Story.*—Jonah is known to have been a historical character, being identified by almost all scholars with "Jonah the son of Amittai," who prophesied to Jeroboam the restoration of Israel to their ancient boundaries, II Kings 14:25. Sellin states without hesitation or modification, "The hero of the narrative is a *historical personage,* who lived in the time of Jeroboam II, shortly before Amos." Their identification seems assured, as both Jonah's name and that of his father occur nowhere else in the entire Old Testament. He was a native of Gath-hepher in Galilee, which is situated about four miles north of Nazareth, and is known to the modern Arabs as el-Meshed, II Kings 14:25.

When called by Jehovah to go to Nineveh and preach, the task was so repugnant to him that he fled "from the presence of the Lord," Jonah 1:3,

70

10, to Tarshish, i.e., Tartessus, in southwestern Spain, resigning his prophetic work. Pusey feels that Jonah at this time was already well advanced in life, having probably stood "in the presence of the Lord" for years. Cain, also, went out "from the presence of the Lord," Gen. 4:16; Jonah was a true Cain-ite!

In the sequel of the story, he frankly gives his reason for going westward, hazarding the sea which the Hebrews usually avoided, instead of eastward. "For I knew that thou art a gracious God, and merciful, slow to anger, and abundant in loving kindness, and repentest thee of the evil," 4:2. Doubtless he would have gone to Nineveh had he been sure that God would really destroy the city. But being a narrow patriot, jealous and vindictive, he could not see why God should wish him to preach to a people who stood eager to devour Israel. The true Christian, on the other hand, desires the welfare even of his enemies, Luke 6:27, 28.

Going down to Joppa, the chief seaport of the Holy Land, he found a vessel sailing far westward; going on board, he paid the fare thereof, descended into the hold, and fell asleep, as Sisera in the tent of the treacherous Jael, Judg. 4:21. His conscience also slept, for he had deceived himself into thinking that he would soon be far away from God. Jesus likewise slept peacefully during a storm; but as Marti suggests, "confident not because he felt himself far *from* God's hand, but because he was hidden *in* God's hand," Mark 4:35-41. When one sets out to baffle God, there is bound to be a storm!

The sea ran high. The sailors prayed, each to his own god; but the storm continued. Some god,

they concluded, must be offended. The shipmaster
finds Jonah and bids him to pray to his God; but,
alas, Jonah really had no God! The sailors, persuaded that there must be a culprit on board the
vessel, cast lots, and the lot fell on Jonah. They
questioned him earnestly concerning his country, his
occupation, and his people, and he frankly confessed
that he was fleeing "from the presence of the Lord."
At that moment he was the only heathen on the
ship! But he quite redeemed himself when he volun-
teered to be thrown overboard for their sakes. The
sailors were loath, however, to offer him as a human
sacrifice, until they had themselves first consulted
Jonah's God; so they prayed that Jehovah would
not lay upon them innocent blood, and *per necessi-
tatem* cast him into the sea, and the storm subsided,
1:14, 15. Thereupon the sailors were so impressed
that they offered a sacrifice to Jehovah and made
vows, 1:16.

Two brief verses sum up the story of his rescue,
1:17; 2:10. Jehovah prepared "a great fish" to
swallow Jonah, and Jonah was in the belly of the fish
"three days and three nights." Two pillars near
Alexandretta, north of Antioch on the coast of
Syria, mark the spot where, according to Arab tradition, Jonah was vomited out on dry land; Josephus,
however, says it was on the shores of the Euxine.

But Jonah, having learned his kinship with
heathen sailors, was given another chance to go
and preach to the heathen of Nineveh. This time
he obeyed; thus becoming as Dean Stanley calls
him: "the first apostle to the Gentiles."

Entering the streets of Nineveh, he began to cry,
perhaps in his own vernacular, "Yet forty days and

Nineveh shall be overthrown"; in Hebrew only five words, 3:4. With what pleasure the revengeful prophet announced this warning, we can only imagine. One prefers to think of him, however, as having uttered these solemn words as a stern preacher, with a boldness worthy of a Nathan, II Sam. 12:7; of a Paul, Acts 24:25; or of a Luther, whose burning truth withered hostile hearts. In similar monotony, doubtless John the Baptist at a later time, repeated his prophetic call, "Repent ye, for the kingdom of heaven is at hand," Matt. 3:2. Jonah spoke but five words—words of doom at that—but their effect was electric; the Ninevites repented, and as a consequence, God also "repented of the evil which he said he would do unto them; and he did it not," 3:5-10.

At Jehovah's delay in executing judgment upon the wicked city, Jonah became vexed. He was vexed, not because he felt discredited in the eyes of the men of Nineveh, or because his professional standing as a prophet was ruined by the failure of his prediction, but because of God's clemency toward Nineveh; being willing to spare a city which would only continue to harass and decimate Israel through war and the exaction of heavier and ever heavier tribute. In short, Jonah was vexed because of a narrow, selfish patriotism with which he was obsessed. For, he keenly felt that God was losing an opportunity, and that in consequence his own people would be sooner or later doomed to destruction. "Better to die, therefore," he felt, "than to live any longer in a world governed by such a God!" In his despondency Jonah resembles Elijah, I Kings 19:1-18. But there was a difference between them: Jonah "was depressed with Elijah's despondency, but without Elijah's excuse"; the difference between them being, as G. A. Smith has pointed out, that "Elijah was jealous *for* God; Jonah was jealous *of* God."

Jonah waited to see the city destroyed, watching the issue of things from a scorching hilltop on the east of Nineveh. Jehovah remonstrated with him because of his anger, but without avail. To protect him from the fierce heat of the semi-tropical sun, God caused to grow up over his head, with almost magical swiftness, a bottle-gourd, a *ricinus communis*. Jonah was greatly pleased. But, quite as swiftly God allowed it to wither, gnawed by a worm; "the son of a night," 4:10. Because of this fatal calamity to the gourd, Jonah became not only angry, but sullen and morose, even wishing himself to die, 4:9. He had been angry, at first, because Nineveh *was spared;* he is now angry because the gourd *was not spared*. Jehovah responds, contrasting the gourd and the city, and commenting on their mutual regard and solicitation for each; and the story is at an end!

Now, whatever may be our estimate of the *book* of Jonah, and its value cannot easily be overestimated, it must be allowed that Jonah himself stands relatively very low in the catalogue of Old Testament prophets. Because, Jonah was a proud, self-centered egotist: wilful, fretful, pouting and perverse! Yet withal, a good patriot, and a loyal lover of Israel! As a preacher, he was probably as good as the average run of preachers to-day; for, who of us never rejoiced when in war the enemy lost their choicest soldiers? Jonah was jealous of the Ninevites, but scarcely more so than we are of our national foes, or of the heathen.   The Judaists of apostolic times certainly begrudged the gospel being offered by Paul to the Gentiles on equal terms with themselves.   Whether Jonah's attitude toward Nineveh changed as the result of Jehovah's final remonstrance, we are not told; but so far as we are informed, Jonah was a revengeful, blood-thirsty, prophet-patriot, who preached with wonderful, even extraordinary success, yet without being able to see that he had succeeded.

In the last analysis, Jonah was a man in whom piety and duty were ever in conflict; a man who feared God, but at the same time ran away from his task, 1:3, 9; a man in whom the spirit of humanity had been almost killed out by patriotism; in short, a man whose religion resided in the realm of emotion, rather than in the sphere of the will. Jesus, in contrast, wept over Jerusalem!

II. *The Prophet's Times.*—Jonah lived, as we know, during the reign of Jeroboam II, king of North Israel, who reigned from about 790 to 750 B.C.   Jeroboam found the kingdom weak for the reason that ever since the time of Jehu, his great-grandfather, the people had been forced to pay continual tribute to Assyria.   Under Jeroboam, however, the people began to revive their former strength.   He captured Hamath and Damascus and restored to Israel all the territory stretching southward from Hamath to the Dead Sea, as Jonah had predicted, II Kings 14:25.   Jeroboam, indeed, was the most powerful of all the monarchs that ever sat upon the throne of Samaria, and the kingdom's future was most hopeful.

In Assyria, on the contrary, the prevailing conditions were just the opposite: everything was most discouraging, Assyria was losing ground. In other words, Israel was in the ascendancy, Assyria was on the decline. The brilliant reign of Adadnirari IV, *ca.* 810-782, B.C. had just closed. In his three expeditions to Palestine and the West Lands, he had received tribute from the Hittites, Tyre and Sidon, "the land of Omri," i.e., North Israel, Edom, and Philistia, and through his extensive victories had made himself one of the greatest kings Assyria ever had. "No Assyrian king before him had actually ruled over so wide an extent of territory, and none had ever possessed, in addition to this, so extensive a circle of tribute-paying states" (So, R. W. Rogers, *Hist. of Babylonia and Assyria*, II, 258). It was Adadnirari IV who advocated, like Amenhophis IV of Egypt's Eighteenth Dynasty, a kind of religious monotheism, and who left a rather remarkable inscription which reads: "Put thy trust in Nebo; trust not another god." Winckler suggests that it was Adadnirari, who as "king of Nineveh," welcomed Jonah when he came to Nineveh to preach. But it is more probable that Adadnirari was now dead, and that Assyria's decline had already begun; for, as Rogers points out, "after his reign there comes slowly but surely a period of strange, almost inexplicable, decline" (*Ibid.*, pp. 258-259). It was this appearance of decline that made Jonah wish to see Assyria decline still more!

A difficulty, however, arises just here, because of the fact that at this particular time and down until the time of Sennacherib in 705 B.C., Calah, and not Nineveh, was the capital of Assyria. But the difficulty is easily explained when it is recalled that

Calah and Nineveh were really only different names
for essentially the same city, being less than twenty
miles apart; and that Nineveh is not called in the
Book of Jonah the actual "capital" of Assyria. According to Ctesias and Diodorus, "Nineveh may
have denoted a province," namely, "the Assyria
proper between the four rivers." The actual extent
of the city, Diodorus tells us, was about 1,800 acres.
In any case we know that Nineveh was an ancient
city, having been founded by Nimrod, Gen. 10:11;
and that it is twice mentioned in the Tell el-Amarna
letters, which antedate Jonah's times by some eight
hundred years. The monuments inform us also that
its people were among the most violent and cruel
of all the nations of antiquity. It was to such a
city, therefore, and in times that were most discouraging for Assyria, but not for Israel, that Jonah
was commissioned to preach.

III. *Analysis.*—The chapter divisions mark the
natural divisions of the book:

Chapter 1, Jonah's disobedience; "running away
from God."

Chapter 2, His prayer; "running to God."

Chapter 3, His preaching to Nineveh; "running
with God."

Chapter 4, His complaints; "running ahead of
God."

IV. *The Two Great Miracles.*—Both are char-
acteristically Oriental.

1. *The Great Fish.*—No other story in the Bible
has probably caused so much jeering allusion, silly
derision, ribald mockery, and blundering exegesis as
"the story of Jonah and the whale!" With Moore,
"it might almost be said that the sea-monster has

swallowed the commentators as well as the prophet."
The details of a comparatively trivial incident have
been unduly magnified; supreme emphasis being
placed on things in which supreme values do not
exist.   Some expositors have been so ill-advised as
to make belief in the marvel of the fish a test of
orthodoxy.   But it was probably the last purpose
of the author that we should pore over the whale
and forget God!   In a very true sense, however, the
intrusion of "the fish" into the solemnities of the
story is no ridiculous thing; for that fish was the
making of a prophet!

The question is not whether a fish can be found
large enough to swallow a man without mutilation.
Giant white sharks and the sperm whale, technically
known as the *catodon macrocephalus,* have been captured which could swallow not only a little, "Minor"
prophet like Jonah, but a "Major"; even horses!
For example, that captured off Knight's Key,
Florida, in 1912, and now on exhibition in the
Smithsonian Institute at Washington, D. C., measured 45 feet in length, had a mouth 38 inches wide,
and weighed 30,000 pounds, having in its stomach
at the time of capture a black fish which weighed
approximately 1,500 pounds.

Of far greater importance is the question, How
was the prophet sustained alive in the belly of any
fish "three days"?   Analogies are sometimes cited
and explanations given.   For example, the case of a
sailor, who in 1758, fell overboard in the Mediterranean and was picked up by a shark, which, in turn,
on being hit by a cannon ball, disgorged him un-
harmed; or, that of an Indian who was swallowed
by a shark and found still alive after the animal was

captured and opened, though he soon afterward died. The late Professor Macloskie of Princeton, explained Jonah's particular case by supposing that the prophet "found lodgment in the laryngeal chamber of the whale, where he could breathe, rather than in its stomach, where he must have been suffocated"!

But all such apologetic explanations of the phenomenon are trifling and unworthy; for, either the story is history, and, therefore, a genuine miracle, or it is an oriental story with no foundation of fact either intended or implied. The statement that Jonah was in the belly of the fish "three days and three nights," 1:17, is an oriental way of expressing the fact that he was in the fish so long that apart from God's sustaining power, he was dead and beyond the possibility of human resuscitation, cf. John 11:17. The author, we may be sure, intended to portray Jonah's preservation from death, or return to life, as supernatural.

2. *The conversion of Nineveh.*—This is the greater wonder of the two. That of the fish was physical; this is moral. To many, the thought of a great city, repenting suddenly at the preaching of a Hebrew stranger is incredible, even unthinkable. Nineveh was the London of Jonah's day, having been built upon the spoils of war. It was populous, having it is estimated not fewer than 600,000 inhabitants, 4:11; it was also opulent, proud and well fortified; its walls, according to Diodorus, being 100 feet high. Included within its area were parks and gardens, possibly even pasture lands, for the "much cattle" therein, 4:11. It is described as "a city great unto God," 3:3 Mg., a phrase which expresses

the devout habit of the Hebrew mind which recognizes God in everything. The implication is that Jonah was commissioned to preach to no mean city, and that his was a man's task!

Nineveh is also described as a city "of three days' journey." This is a decidedly oriental expression. It has nothing to do with the diameter or the circumference of the city, which Diodorus describes as 480 *stadia,* i.e., about 60 miles; oriental cities are usually built very compactly; but it refers rather to the fact that "three days" would be required to visit and see all its principal points of interest. For example, ask a native of Palestine to-day, as the present writer once did in Nazareth, "Which city, Nazareth or Beirut, is the better?" and the answer will be returned quickly, "Oh, Beirut is a city of three days"! referring to its superior size.

Entering Nineveh, "a day's journey," Jonah began to preach, and by his stern, cryptic message of repentance, universal panic was at once produced. For the first time in Nineveh's history, probably, "Wisdom cried aloud in her streets," Prov. 1:20. We shall never be able to understand the magical, almost tragical, effect of his message until we appreciate the earnestness with which he, as an Oriental, delivered it; and also, the psychological temper of the Ninevites. Jonah bore in his countenance the glow of the supernatural. After his experience in the sea, he probably preached like one raised from the dead. His face doubtless shone, like Moses', with the glory of God; his eye flashed, his brow was knit, and his lips trembled as he shouted, "Yet forty days and Nineveh shall be overthrown!" Macaulay characterized Demosthenes' oratory as "reason made red hot by passion." Jonah's was surcharged with the thunderings and lightnings of Divine oratory. The prophet had died, as it were, and been brought back to life again. It sometimes requires an experience akin to Jonah's to make a good preacher!

The Ninevites being ignorant and superstitious, especially at this particular period when rebellion was chronic in many of their provinces, and the city was constantly in peril from besiegers who might appear before her gates at any signal, were easily stricken with awe. Orientals generally can be easily stirred to a pitch of frenzy by the announcement of some impending judgment that is feared. Thus, Belshazzar was terrified by the handwriting on the wall, Dan. 5 :5, 6. Likewise Herod the Great, at the announcement of the Magi, "was troubled and all Jerusalem with him," Matt. 2 :3. Layard, the archæologist, tells how a Christian priest once frightened a whole Moslem town by announcing an earthquake. Four years before the destruction of Jerusalem in A.D. 70, an unlettered rustic, named Jesus ben Anan, burst in on the people at the feast of tabernacles with the oft-repeated cry: "A voice from the East, a voice from the West, a voice from the four winds, a voice on Jerusalem and the temple, a voice on the bridegrooms and the brides, a voice on the whole people"; and the city was terribly terrified. And it is known through the ancient records, that shortly before Nineveh's actual collapse, the rulers of the city ordered a solemn fast for one hundred days beseeching the sun-god to forgive their sins.

So, Jonah's solemn, imperious warning, uttered in

tones of fierce and impetuous earnestness, as Peter's
brief sermon on the day of Pentecost, awakened the
slumbering consciences of the Ninevites and they
became panicstricken through fear of impending
calamity; and accordingly they proclaimed a fast,
put on sackcloth, and believed "God"—not "Jehovah," 3:5. When the king heard what was taking
place in the streets, he, too, was terrified. He, too,
perceived the gravity of the situation, put off his
royal robes—the insignia of authority—and sat in
ashes, and he made proclamation that men and
cattle, both, should also fast and cover themselves
with sackcloth, and cry mightily unto God, 3:5-8.

Such expressions of fear and repentance were
customary among the ancients. Herodotus tells us
how the Persians clipped the hair of their horses
and baggage animals that they might seem to share
in the nation's mourning for a certain general named
Massistius who fell at Platæa. And Xenophon re-
lates that "when news came to Athens of the destruction of her fleet at Ægospotami, the cry and woe
began at the Piræus and ran along the walls of the
city, and on that night no one slept because of sorrow
for the past, terror for the future, and also for
remorse"; because they felt that what was coming
upon them was retribution for their own faithless
and atrocious cruelty to Ægina, to Melos, and to
Scione. The world, after all, is ruled not by truth
but by opinion. A true prophet is never without
allies!

The repentance of the Ninevites, of course, was
not repentance in the Christian sense; it was like
Jonah's on board ship, temporary and superficial,
genuine only to the extent of their intellectual and

religious capacities, and enduring only as long as they were afraid. Their only argument was, who knoweth whether God will not turn and repent of his fierce anger that we perish not, 3:9? The miracle of grace is a miracle indeed!

V. *How Best Interpreted.*—Three views prevail, the mythical, the historical, and the allegorical or parabolic.

1. *The mythical interpretation.*—Simpson assures us that when the book of Jonah is viewed from the standpoint of myth or legend, "then all becomes simple"! According to his interpretation, the mythical neophyte in the book of Jonah receives orders to proceed to Nineveh, but disobeys and takes a ship for Tarshish, when, in the author's imagination, a storm breaks, and the initiate is lowered into the sea, i.e., into sheol or the grave, the fish being a figure for "the belly of hell," 2:2; but after three days he is brought up again and restored to life. This Simpson claims is analogous to numerous other ancient tales and rituals, in which simulated death is followed by a re-birth into what was considered a new person or another life, the novitiate oftentimes forgetting everything that he had previously known. The Eleusinian Mysteries, in which the history of Demeter and Cora was acted as a play by priests and priestesses, were of this same initiatory type, a sort of "mystical drama." Initiatory rites were thus regenerative in their symbolism. The story of Jonah, according to Simpson, was an initiatory legend; the very name, "Jonah," which means "Dove," being to him strong evidence of the mythical character of the prophet, as Aphrodite, to whom the dove was sacred, came out of the sea! In like

manner, the Exodus of the Israelites from the land
of Egypt, Simpson shows, was an initiatory legend;
so also the resurrection; likewise Solomon, who was
a fish god; and the Greater "Prince of Peace" who
was a Fish, ΙΧΘΥΣ, being the mystical name of
Christ. For evidence, Simpson appeals to Augustine, who says, "he descended alive into the depths
of this mortal life, as into the abyss of waters"; but
especially to Tertullian who explicitly says, "We are
little fishes in Christ, our great fish. For we are
born in water and can only be saved therein."
There is much, confessedly, that is attractive in this
view of the book of Jonah, but Simpson's interpretation is really too "simple" to be convincing!

2. *The historical interpretation.*—According to
this interpretation, the story of Jonah is historically
true, being based upon the facts of the prophet's actual experience. In substantiation of this view
several important considerations have weight; thus
(a) the form of the book itself, which is that of
simple historical narrative, and was so regarded by
both Jews and Christians till about a century ago.
(b) The book of Tobit, 14:4, 8, dating from the
second century B.C.; the Book of III Maccabees,
6:8, dating from the first century B.C.; and the *An-
tiquities* of Josephus, ix, 10, 2, written toward the
close of the first century, A.D.—all treat of Jonah's
call and preaching to Nineveh as an actual fact. (c)
Jonah was not the only Old Testament prophet who
ministered to foreign nations; compare Elijah's mission to Sarepta, I Kings 17:8 ff., and Elisha's to Damascus, II Kings 8:7 ff.; cf. also Hos. 5:13. (d)
Most modern critics agree that there is a kernel of
history at the bottom of the Jonah story, that at least

Jonah did at one time actually preach to Nineveh.
(e) Add to this the analogous experience of the
prophet Hosea, which until recent years was regarded as an allegory, but which critics now almost
universally explain as a part of Hosea's actual
domestic experience, Hos. 1-3, and the shipwreck of
Jonah finds a tragic parallel. Indeed, both prophets
were "called" through most marvelous providences
of God!

3. *The allegorical or parabolic interpretation.*—
This view rests upon the conviction that though
there are genuine miracles in the Bible, God is not
accustomed to perform the kind of miracles described in the book of Jonah. For, if the story is
literally true, then Jonah's success eclipses that of
all other Old Testament prophets, even Elijah's
victory on Mount Carmel, I Kings, chapter 18.
And if the story is literally true, then why are certain historical details such as the sins of Nineveh,
the name of Nineveh's king, the size of the city, and
the effect of God's rebuke upon Jonah passed over in
silence?

Accordingly, it is argued that Jonah is more than
a mere individual in history, he is a human type, a
historico-symbolical prophet; and that the facts of
the story are of less importance than the lessons
they teach; in fact, that in Jonah "we are in won-
derland," and that the story is poetry not prose,
resembling in character the Book of Job, the parables of the Prodigal Son and the Good Samaritan,
Lessing's Ring Story in *Nathan the Wise,* Oscar
Wilde's *The Teacher of Truth,* and Bunyan's *Pil-
grim's Progress;* and bearing everywhere upon it
the signs of allegory, symbol, and parable.

Thus, Jonah stands as the representative of Israel; the fish, as Israel's captivity in Babylon; the vomiting of Jonah upon dry land, as Israel's return from captivity, etc. Nebuchadnezzar, indeed, is actually described in Jer. 51:34,44 as having "swallowed" up Israel, cf. Hos. 6:1, 2. There are also many other allegories in the Old Testament, it is urged, e.g., that of Nathan to David, II Sam. 12:1-7, that of the woman of Tekoa, II Sam. 14:1-20, that of the prisoner let loose, by an anonymous prophet to Ahab, I Kings 20:39-41, and others.

But there are two serious, if not fatal, objections to this interpretation: (a) No other allegory in the entire Old Testament has as its hero *an historical person*. Modern novelists may produce what we call historical fiction; but so far as we know the ancient Hebrews never did. Besides, the author would hardly have condemned a guiltless prophet of Jeroboam's time to such lasting ignominy unless there was some substantial historical foundation for the story. Dummelow's attempt to find a parallel in the New Testament parable of the Pounds, which he assumes is based upon the well-known incidents of the visits of Herod the Great and Archælaus to Rome, is suggestive of the fact that Jonah has no analogy. The parable of Dives and Lazarus, and the reference in it to "Abraham's bosom," is equally unconvincing for the reason that the phrase "Abraham's bosom" does not make Abraham the hero of the parable; it was rather the common appellation in Christ's day for "paradise" or "heaven." If the book of Jonah is an allegory or parable, therefore, the hero of the story cannot well have been the historical Jonah of II Kings 14:25. Better assume that the hero, too, is parabolic! Budde evidently felt the force of this argument; for he explains the book as a "Midrash," suggested indeed by II Kings 14:25, but originally belonging to the larger "book of kings" mentioned in II Chron. 24:27. (b) The other objection to this interpretation is the presence in it of *the miraculous*. Anything miraculous is directly contrary to the very genius of the allegory, or parable. By nature parables and allegories stand opposed to everything grotesque or unbelievable. In them the thought and fact are one, and the truth is easily accepted, because self-evident. The story of the fish, therefore, and of the conversion of the Ninevites, completely vitiate the nature of a parable, or allegory, as we know them in the Bible.

VI. *Our Lord's Use of Jonah.*—Twice in the Synoptists Jesus is reported to have been asked by the Scribes and Pharisees to give them a sign, and twice he responded by citing to them the case of the prophet Jonah and his preaching to Nineveh, Matt. 12:38-42; 16:4; Luke 11:29-32. Possibly our Lord's use of the book will assist us in interpreting it. Strange that so many modern expositors quite ignore this possibility! We naturally ask two questions: (a) Of what did the Scribes and Pharisees seek a sign? Of his character, mission, messianic claims, his right as a Jew to preach a world-wide redemption on the basis of repentance? or what? and (b) in what sense did he mean that no sign would be given them save that of the prophet Jonah?

The summary of our Lord's answer seems to be, "As Jonah preached repentance to all men, including Gentiles, so do I; as Jonah had to die, as it

were, before he was used of God in the accomplish-
ment of his mission, so do I; as he died in a very
true sense, vicariously, for his own people, so must
I; the men of Nineveh, however, responded to
Jonah's message of repentance, but you pay no heed
to mine; therefore, they will rise up in the judgment and condemn you, for you have far more going
on around you than they had, to shut you up to
repentance." Thus, Jesus rebukes the Scribes and
Pharisees for insisting on external proof; external
signs, he knew, seldom convince men who have no
light within themselves. Jonah himself did no
miracle.

But the question which chiefly concerns us is this:
Did our Lord use the Book of Jonah as history, or
as parable, or as something else? In the same connection he goes on to speak of the Queen of the
South, how she came "from the ends of the earth,
to hear the wisdom of Solomon, and behold a
greater than Solomon is here"; and it certainly
seems unlikely that he would mingle real and ficti-
tious names in the same context. If the account of
the Queen of the South were history, and the story
of Jonah were fiction, Jesus surely might have dis-
criminated between them in the interests of intellectual honesty.

But to deny the historicity of the book of Jonah
by no means involves denial of Christ and his resurrection. The whole matter is in a very true sense
a question of interpretation rather than of faith.
We surely cannot take all Jesus said about Jonah
au pied de la lettre. For example, Jesus was not
literally "three days and three nights in the heart
of the earth," Matt. 12:40. Let us not quibble

over this difficult passage. Jesus often used great latitude in interpreting the Old Testament; and he frequently spoke in parables himself; hence he may have pointed to the deep symbolism of the book of Jonah as of the same sort. On one occasion he even foretold his own violent death by means of a parable—that of the wicked husbandman who said of the heir, "Come let us kill him and take his inheritance," Matt. 21:38. Obviously, his chief point in citing Jonah as a sign to the Pharisees was, that Jonah's three days in the belly of the fish and the repentance of the Ninevites stand *in the relation of cause and effect;* and that as Jonah died and rose again and then preached with success, so the Son of Man must die and rise before men will believe on him. Orelli catches the true significance of our Lord's reference when he says: "Whoever, therefore, feels the religious greatness of the book, and accepts as authoritative the attitude taken to its historical import by the Son of God himself, will be led to accept a great act of the God who brings down to Hades and brings up again, as an actual experience of Jonah in his flight from his Lord."

VII. *Permanent Teaching.*—The author of the book of Jonah strikes the high-water mark of Old Testament theology. In large heartedness, in love of mankind, and in the appreciation of the character of God, this little book stands preëminent as the noblest, broadest, and most Christian of all Old Testament literature. It contains one truth far in advance of Jonah's age, a truth which will never pass out of date so long as men have human hearts, and prize the gospel. According to Jerome, Cyprian was converted by it, "sermonem Ionae audiisse et ad

Deum conversum." Cornill testifies that he "cannot take up this marvelous book, or even speak of it, without the tears rising in his eyes." Sellin regards it as "one of the most precious jewels of Hebrew literature!" Among the great truths suggested by it are these:

1. *The catholicity of divine grace.*—This is the chief lesson of the book. The author reserves it to the end, 4:10,11; and with it stops, to give it emphasis. It is the Old Testament counterpart to John 3:16, "For God so loved the world." Terence expressed a famous and oft-quoted dictum akin to that taught by the book of Jonah when he said, "I am a man, and to myself hold nothing foreign that is human"; but the author of Jonah tells us rather what *God* thinks of the masses. Like a great missionary statesman, he anticipates the catholicity of the gospel program of Jesus. To the author of Jonah God is no mere tribal deity; the heathen as well as the seed of Abraham are included in the Divine election,

> "For the love of God is broader
>   Than the measure of man's mind,
> And the heart of the Eternal
>   Is most wonderfully kind."

As Theodoret observed, "The book of Jonah foreshadows the preaching of the gospel far and wide over the whole earth." It surely discovers the soul of the Bible, and makes its own silent appeal for foreign missions.

2. *A higher patriotism.*—Over against the narrow patriotism of the mean and contemptible little spirit

of Jonah, who was a mirror for the nation, the author gives us, as we have already seen, a picture of the loving, fatherly, catholic God. The comparison was meant to sting Israel to the quick for their bigotry and hardness of heart. It was an unconscious rebuke to the spirit of the "elder brother" in the as yet unuttered parable of the Prodigal Son. Jonah was intensely patriotic, but he was also jealous and revengeful. His patriotism was of the common type, base and low, and therefore false. The patriotism of many Christians is no better.

George Adam Smith tells of the awful hatred of the infidel Turk by the oriental churches in Turkey to-day. He says, "For centuries they have had no spiritual intercourse with them; to try to convert a Mohammedan has been for twelve hundred years a capital crime. Once I asked a cultured and devout layman of the Greek Church, Why, then, did God create so many Mohammedans? The answer came hot and fast, 'To fill up Hell!'" But this spirit is by no means confined to the Orient. On the other hand, true patriotism, the higher patriotism, the patriotism taught in the book of Jonah, includes other nations, and heathen peoples, too.

3. *The conditional character of prophecy,* . . . especially of God's threatenings. Ewald made this the main purpose of the book, namely, to teach that when God threatens, his threatenings are always conditional. The book furnishes a practical illustration of Jer. 18:7, 8, and Ezekiel, chapter 33. The Ninevites felt, as we are entitled to feel, that when God threatens he is promising; that when he comes near in any way it is for our salvation; or, as the older theologians used to say, that God is not

obliged to fulfill his threats, but he is obliged to fulfill his promises. The awakened conscience instinctively feels that threatenings cannot be God's last words to it, but must have been given that they might not need to be fulfilled; that, judgment, indeed, through repentance, may be exchanged for salvation.

4. *The secret of effective preaching.*—The book has a special lesson for preachers. It teaches that to be an effective preacher, one must first die, so to speak, like Jonah, and rise again. *Via crucis, via lucis:* "the way of the cross, the way of light." This is the law of effective prophecy the world over. People are most easily won to repentance and to God through vicarious sacrifice. Jonah, though a very imperfect example of what a Christian preacher ought to be, illustrates this principle. Every true Christian preacher must have in his heart room for all mankind.

5. *The necessity for obedience.*—Obedience is the most obvious lesson in the book. Jonah attempted to run away "from the presence of the Lord." But men cannot escape their divinely appointed destiny, nor shirk God's will in their lives. As Riehm points out, it is wrong in a prophet, as it is also useless, to evade a duty once imposed.

VIII. *Canonicity.*—Kirkpatrick, in his *Doctrine of the Prophets,* excludes the Book of Jonah, "because it is not a record of a prophet's *teaching* but the account of a prophet's *work*"; but he does not exclude it from the Canon. There is no evidence whatever, "to show that the recognition of Jonah as a book of canonical scripture was ever seriously imperilled" (so Ryle, *The Canon of the Old Testa-*

ment, p. 194). Its spirit and teaching are not only on a par with, but far above the spirit and teaching of most, even the greatest, of Old Testament prophets. It was, therefore, a true instinct which led the collectors to include this book and place it among the prophets. König assays to explain its exact place among the Twelve, immediately following Obadiah, as due to a phrase with which the latter opens, namely, "and an ambassador is sent among the nations," Obad. 1:1; Jonah was that ambassador and the Book of Jonah has consequently been sometimes called "God's Commentary on Obadiah." The Jews read it on the Great Day of Atonement.

SPECIAL LITERATURE ON JONAH

Kalisch, "The Book of Jonah," *Bible Studies*, II (1878); Kennedy, *The Book of Jonah* (1895); William Simpson, *The Jonah Legend* (1899); Townsend, *The Story of Jonah* (1887); Hutton, *The Persistent Word of God* (1918); Redford, *Studies in the Book of Jonah; a Defense and Exposition* (1883); Trumbull, "Jonah in Nineveh," *Journal of Biblical Literature* (1892); Dale, "Jonah," *Expositor* (1892); Kohler, "The Original Form of the Book of Jonah," *Theological Review* (1879); Briggs, "Works of the Imagination in the Old Testament," *North American Review* (1897); Cheyne, "Jonah: A Study in Jewish Folklore and Religion," *Theological Review* (1887); Döller, *Das Buch Jona* (1912); Böhme, "Die Komposition des Buches Jona," *ZATW* (1887); H. Schmidt, "Absicht und Entstehungszeit des Buches Jona," *Theol. Stud u. Kritiken* (1906).

CHAPTER VI

MICAH THE PROPHET OF THE POOR

I. *Name.*—Micah, the sixth of the Twelve, bore
a name which in itself was a creed, the fuller and
probably older form, *Mikâyâhu,* signifying "who is
like unto Jehovah?" (Mic. 1:1; 7:18; Jer. 26:18).
Like Michael, meaning "who is like unto God?" the
name contains a challenge. Our prophet should not
be confounded with Micah ben Imlah, whom Ahab
hated (I Kings 22:8).

II. *Home.*—He is called "the Morashtite" (Mic.
1:1), having been born in Moresheth-gath (1:14),
a dependence of Gath, about 20 miles distant southwest of Jerusalem. Jerome locates Moresheth definitely a little east of Eleutheroplis, the modern
Beit-Jibrin. Like Amos, he was a native of the
country. There is usually more home religion in
the country than in the city. Micah apparently had
no special love for *cities* (1:5; 5:11; 6:9).

III. *Personality.*—Micah must have been a very
striking personality. Possessed of strong convic-
tions, he showed corresponding courage. The secret
of his power is told in 3:8, "But as for me, I am full
of power by the Spirit of Jehovah, and of judgment,
and of might, to declare unto Jacob his transgres-
sion, and to Israel his sin." As a true patriot and
like every true preacher, he fearlessly uncovered sin

and pointed to Christ. He was preëminently a
prophet of the poor and a friend of the oppressed.
His whole soul went out in loyal sympathy to the
downtrodden. "He had Amos' passion for justice
and Hosea's heart of love" (J. M. P. Smith).
Micah was Amos *redivivus*. His unfeigned sincerity stands out in sharp contrast to the flattering
teachings of his contemporaries, who, as false
prophets, regulated their messages by their income
(3:5).

IV. *Times.*—According to the title of his book,
Micah prophesied "in the days of Jotham, Ahaz,
and Hezekiah, kings of Judah" (1:1), a date amply
confirmed by internal evidence, and also by Jer.
26:18, which quotes Mic. 3:12. Micah, accordingly, was a younger contemporary of Isaiah. More
explicitly, he seems to have preached both before
and after the downfall of Samaria (722 B.C.), very
probably from about 735 till 715 B.C.; Mackay
thinks "over forty years." Under Jotham splendid
luxury reigned. His ambition to build fortresses
and palaces in Jerusalem cost many a peasant's life.
Under Ahaz, Judah was forced to pay tribute to
Assyria, which, together with the cost of the Syro-
Ephraimitic war of 734 B.C., fell as a heavy burden
upon all classes. Both rich and poor suffered. The
grasping, avaricious landlords used their power to
oppress, confiscating the property of the poor and
even evicting widows from their houses. All sorts
of economic crimes were perpetrated, the plutocrats
devouring the humbler classes as "sheep crop grass."
Under Hezekiah, who attempted to reform the
state, conditions became even more hopeless. Men
ceased to trust one another, Jerusalem became a

hotbed of factions and intrigue. The advisers of
the king became divided in their policies, some
urging alliance with Egypt against Assyria, others
submission to Assyria. The custodians of the law
abused their powers; nobles fleecing the poor, judges
accepting of bribes, prophets flattering the rich, and
priests teaching for hire (chap. 2). Lust of wealth
ruled on all sides. The moneyed tyrants laughed
at possible judgment. Commercialism and mate-
rialism were supplanting almost the last vestige of
everything ethical and spiritual. At such a crisis
Micah appeared and attempted to call the nation
back to God and to duty. Sellin feels that 3:11, 12
would be more intelligible after the centralization
of the cultus which Hezekiah undertook.

V. *Message.*—Micah's message supplemented
Isaiah's. They were contemporaries. Isaiah was
a courtier, Micah a rustic from an obscure village.
Isaiah was a statesman; Micah an evangelist and
a sociologist. Isaiah addressed himself to political
issues; Micah dealt almost exclusively with personal
religion and social morality. He was more demo-
cratic than Isaiah. His personal relationship was
not with kings, but with the people. He was a
prophet of the people. Isaiah taught the inviola-
bility of Zion; Micah predicted her destruction
(3:12). The nobility had a totally mistaken conception of God. They fancied that because they
were respectable judgment was impossible. "Is not
Jehovah in the midst of us?" they asked, "no evil
shall come upon us" (3:11). Micah possessed advanced ideas of the kingdom of God and raised the
standard of religion and ethics very high (6:8).
His whole message might almost be summed up in

this one sentence: Those who live selfish and luxurious lives, even though they offer costly sacrifices, are vampires in the sight of God, sucking the life-blood of the poor. His words fairly quiver with feeling.

VI. *Analysis.*—Despite the thrice-repeated formula, "Hear ye" (1:2; 3:1; 6:1), which introduces the three main sections of the book, the best division of the material, according to the character of the subject-matter, is as follows: chaps. 1-3, judgment; chaps. 4-5, comfort; chaps. 6-7, the *via salutis,* or way of salvation,—a model outline for even a modern sermon!

1. *Chapters 1-3.*—Sharp denunciation and unrelieved doom; full of impassioned invectives against the officers of church and state, accompanied by peals of judgment, menace, and threatening, until the prophet's censures are no longer welcome and his auditors bid him stop (2:6). Micah was the first of the prophets to threaten Jerusalem with destruction (3:12): but the fate of *the nation* he kept clear and distinct from the fate of *the capital.* His threats are followed happily with promises of restoration.

2. *Chapters 4-5.*—Glimpses of coming glory, with promises of salvation, including messianic and eschatological hopes. Micah looks backward as well as forward. As always in the Old Testament, his vision of the future is founded upon the actualities of the present. In the coming deliverance of Judah, perhaps from Sennacherib (701 B.C.), he sees the future triumph of righteousness. Two pictures flash across his mind, the exaltation of Zion and the Messiah's birth in Bethlehem:

(a) Chapter 4:1-5 is a picture of Zion, destined,

he sees, to become the spiritual metropolis of the whole world (cf. Isa. 2:2-4); pilgrims flocking thither from all quarters forming "a federation of the world" under the suzerainty of the God of Israel; the law of the Lord accepted as their universal arbiter in an age of universal peace; Israel religiously supreme; the long-looked-for golden age, accordingly, becoming a reality.

(b) Chapter 5:2 ff. prophesies that the Messiah is to be born in Bethlehem, as David was. Isaiah had foretold his virgin birth (7:14); Micah predicts his village birth. Seven hundred years later, in the days of Herod the Great, the Magi in search of the spot, through the help of Jewish rabbis, obtained from this passage the direction in which to continue their journey (Matt. 2:1-6).

3. *Chapters 6-7.*—The Lord's controversy, a dialogue exceedingly dramatic, vindicating Jehovah's providence. The people regard God as a hard, grasping, and exacting master, trying to wring out of them unjust requirements. They wish to know, therefore, how much will satisfy him. By cruel and mistaken methods they have been trying to propitiate God, offering the fruit of their bodies for the sins of their souls (6:7). Jehovah responds to them in what is considered by one the greatest saying of the Old Testament, "And what doth Jehovah require of thee, but to do justly, and to love kindness, and to walk humbly with thy God?" (6:8); which Huxley calls "the perfect ideal of religion," embracing at it does the whole duty of man: true worship, true ritual, and true morality. Then the prophet proceeds to give with trenchant force one of the most poignant criticisms of a commercial com-

munity in all literature, denouncing the "scant
measure" (6:10) and the social sins of the nation
which are driving them headlong to doom (6:15,
16). In this section all classes, not the leaders only
as in chaps. 1-3, but the people as a whole, are pronounced bad. There is not a good man left; "The
best of them is as a brier" (7:4). The prophet
concludes with a most beautiful prayer, and a noble
apostrophe to Jehovah, as the incomparable God of
forgiveness and grace (7:7-20).

VII. *The Three Great Texts of Micah.*—

1. *Chapter 3:12.*—"Therefore shall Zion for
your sake be plowed as a field, and Jerusalem shall
become heaps, and the mountain of the house as the
high places of a forest." This text, which is the key-
stone and climax of the prophet's message of judgment, is famous because it was remembered for over
a century, and was the means, literally, of saving
Jeremiah's life (Jer. 26:18). Very rarely does one
prophet in the Old Testament ever cite another.
Evidently Hezekiah's reformation may have been
stimulated to some degree at least by Micah (cf.
II Kings 18:4).

2. *Chapter 5:2.*—"But thou, Bethlehem Ephra-
thah, which art little to be among the thousands of
Judah, out of thee shall one come forth unto me that
is to be ruler in Israel; whose goings forth are from
of old, from everlasting." Micah was the first of all
the prophets to focus men's eyes upon Bethlehem as
the birthplace of a coming Deliverer; a yeoman at
that! He will not be born up there in the capital,
ignorant of rural needs and a foster-brother of the
patricians, but a man of humble origin and a sharer
of the poor man's burdens; in fact, the poor man's

Deliverer. That is to say, Micah, the prophet of the poor, foresaw a poor man's Messiah.

3. *Chapter 6:8.*—"He hath showed thee, O man, what is good; and what doth Jehovah require of thee, but to do justly, and to love kindness, and to walk humbly with thy God?" ¡This verse stands as the motto of the alcove of religion in the reading-room of the Congressional Library in Washington. It contains the three major requirements of all true religion, namely, do justly, love mercy, and walk humbly! Micah thus sums up quite comprehensively in these three phrases the cardinal teachings of the Hebrew religion. The simplification of religion has always been the prophet's vocation. David reduced, as the Talmud suggests, the 613 requirements of the Pentateuch to eleven (Ps. 15); while Micah summed them all up here in three. Jesus, we know, reduced them to two (Matt. 22:35-40). Compare also James' estimate of religious duty when reduced to its lowest terms (Jas. 1:27).

(a) *To do justly:* Justice, in the Bible, is recognized as elementary morality. It is the basis of all moral character, the essential of a good man, one of God's own attributes! No man renders to his fellows all his fellows have a right to expect. The justice here spoken of is not the justice of Shylock, who pertinaciously insisted upon his pound of flesh; nor that of Rob Roy, who maintained that "they should *take* who have the power, and they should *keep* who can." Mere justice is not enough. Rather the ideal justice of the prophet here is the eternal justice of the Golden Rule: "All things therefore whatsover ye would that men should do unto you, even so do ye also unto them; *for this is the law and the prophets"* (Matt. 7:12). The last clause is often overlooked.

(b) *To love kindness (hesed), compassion, mercy:* This is Hosea's favorite word, expressing a higher quality than mere justice. Many fulfill the one, but stop short of the other. Mercy postulates goodness; for while justice implies a debt, kindness implies grace and favor. Kindness, indeed, is the guaranty of justice. If a man does not love a principle he will evade if possible its application. And it is only true to say that "the man who does good, but does not love, is not a good man. He pretends to be, but would be different if he could." God wants not so much ours as us!

"The quality of mercy is not strained,
  It droppeth as the gentle rain from heaven
  Upon the place beneath: it is twice bless'd;
  It blesses him that gives, and him that takes."

(c) *To walk humbly:* This third requirement is a condition of the other two—not a corollary to them. One cannot obey the first two without observing the third. "Shall two walk together except they have agreed?" asks Amos (Amos 3:3). Enoch and Noah walked "with God" (Gen. 5:24; 6:9). A man cannot "walk with" the god of pantheism! "To walk humbly" implies surrender to a Person: "bowing low," as little children. Humility is the greatest ornament of religion.

These three requirements, then, justice, kindness, and humility—fairness, magnanimity, and a lowly heart—are, according to Micah, the three great essentials of a religious life. Christianity does not perceptibly modify them; it only gives them a new

setting and a wider and deeper application. Micah
falls short, as Maclaren observes, only in not telling
of God's power to fulfill these requirements. At
the cross we find the way.

VIII. *Permanent Lessons.*—Micah's influence
was felt, as we have seen, one hundred years later
in Jehoiakim's reign (Jer. 26:18), and his voice has
never since been silenced. Among the many permanent lessons taught by his prophesies are:

1. *Back to Bethlehem* (5:2).—A noteworthy
watchword! To the prophet and to his contemporaries it meant back to David, who conquered the
nation's enemies and secured their peace; to David,
who established a national capital and organized a
central government; to David, who executed judgment and righteousness in the land; to David of
whom Isaiah prophesied "a throne shall be established in loving kindness (Isa. 16:5); to David, of
whom Jeremiah predicted Jehovah would raise up
"a righteous branch" (Jer. 23:5; 33:15); to David,
the constant ideal of the theocracy! The Messiah
of Israel's coming Golden Age, in other words,
would be like David.

To us his message means far more. It means,
back to Jesus Christ, the son of David, who, too,
was born in Bethlehem; to Jesus Christ, the second
and greater David, the Prince of the House of
David; to Jesus Christ, the Savior of mankind both
poor and rich, who was a toiler and a workingman,
who was born in a stable, the son of a peasant girl,
himself a carpenter, who in his parables loves to
speak of the fields and the folds, of the sowers and
the reapers, of the sheep and oxen; who washed the
feet of the disciples, and who bore his own cross;

to Jesus Christ, the friend of humble sinners, for the poor had the gospel preached to them and the common people heard him gladly. Let us be careful not to lift Christ away from the common people!

2. *Back to ethical righteousness* (6:8).—Righteousness was in the Old Testament, and will ever remain, one of the three cardinal virtues of permanent religion. As human nature is always a constant quantity, so the essential requirements of religion are always fundamentally the same. Once and forever Micah brushed aside sacrificial ritual, even the holocaust of a first born, as of trifling importance compared with ethical righteousness. Like Hosea he taught that religion and ethics are inseparable (Hos. 6:6). He also conceived of Israel, that is of the nation, as one gigantic personality which sinned as one and ought to repent as one. He sympathized entirely with the poorer classes. He regarded Jehovah as the spiritual Vindicator of Judah's voiceless sufferers. He looked into the pinched faces of the helpless proletariat, and poured forth the strongest invectives against the landed aristocracy who kept on joining house to house (2:2). He refused to recognize the claims of a would-be nobility. He knew that the land of Israel belonged to Jehovah, and that a Year of Jubilee was needed as a sort of shaking up, to give a new start to all. In thus preaching ethical righteousness Micah anticipated the modern sociologist, and furnished the only possible solution of social discontent. The patricians of his day were self-centered and the plebeians became victimized. Let us take heed lest "the slants" of our lives are too often inwards!

3. *Back to the Prince of Peace.*—"And they shall beat their swords into ploughshares, and their spears into pruning hooks; nation shall not lift up sword against nation, neither shall they learn war any more" (4:3). "This man shall be our peace; when the Assyrian shall come into our land" (5:5). Whether Micah was the first to conceive of the peaceful utopia Zion would some day become, as portrayed in 4:1-5, or borrowed it from another (cf. Isa. 2:2-4), he emphasized the lofty ideal of prophecy which already prevailed in the eighth century B.C., and of the true science of sociology in all time, in which peace, plenty and prosperity are secure. Universal peace, on the basis of law and justice, was the social ideal of the Old Testament; on the basis of the gospel it becomes the expression of brotherly love. Let us not fail at this point!

IX. *Style.*—Vividness and emphasis, lightning flashes of indignation at social wrongs, rapid transitions from threatening to mercy, vehement emotion and sympathetic tenderness, rhetorical force, cadence and rhythm at times elevated and sublime,—these are among the prophet's outstanding literary characteristics. Micah wrote excellent Hebrew. Both his thoughts and his language justify his claim to speak in the power and inspiration of Jehovah (3:8). In 1:10-16 he indulges in a most striking series of puns, some of which Moffat endeavors to bring out in his translation:

Weep *tears* at *Tear*town (Bochim),
grovel in the *dust* at *Dust*town
(Beth-ophrah)

fare forth stripped, O *Fair*town
    (Saphir)!
*Stir*town (Zaanan) dare not *stir*,
Beth-esel . . . . . .
and Maroth hopes in vain;
for doom descends from the Eternal
to the very gates of Jerusalem.

Harness your steeds and away,
    O Horsetown (Lakhish)
O source of Sion's sin,
where the crimes of Israel centre!
O maiden Sion, you must part with
Moresheth of Gath;
and Israel's kings are ever
    balked
at *Balkton* (Achzib).

I will march the conqueror on you yet,
O men of Mareshah;
and Israel's pomp shall perish utterly.
Israel, shave your head and *hair*
in mourning for your children dear,
shave it like a vulture's *bare*,
for they are lost to you.

SPECIAL LITERATURE ON MICAH

T. K. Cheyne, "Micah," *Cambridge Bible* (1882); Articles in *Dictionaries* and *Encyclopædias;* also *O. T. Introductions;* P. Haupt, "The Book of Micah," *Amer. Journal of Semitic Languages and Literatures* (1910); Margolis, *Micah* (1908); H. J. Elhorst, *De Prophetie van Micha*

(1891); von Ryssel, *Untersuchung über die Textgestalt und die Echtheit des Buches Micha* (1887); B. Stade, *ZATW* (1881); K. Budde, "Das Rätsel von Micha I," *ZATW*, 1917-18; W. H. Kosters, "De samenstelling van het boek Micha," *Theologisch Tydschrift* (1893).

CHAPTER VII

NAHUM THE POET

1. *Name.*—Practically nothing is known of the prophet except his name, and even the name does not elsewhere occur in the entire Bible, except in the genealogy of Joseph the foster-father of Jesus (Luke 3:25). Like so many others of the prophets, he is little more than a Voice! Yet the name he bore carried with it a suggestive significance, that of a "Comforter."

II. *Home.*—He is introduced as "Nahum the Elkoshite," a phrase intended probably to designate his birthplace, rather than, as the Targum suggests, his ancestor's name. Compare "Elijah the Tishbite" (I Kings 17:1). The Septuagint speaks of him as "Nahum the Elkesite." Four conjectures have been made as to his home: (1) *Al-Kush,* a village 24 miles north of Mosul, opposite Nineveh, long a seat of the Nestorian Patriarchs, where his tomb is still reverently pointed out by both Christians and Mohammedans, but especially by the resident Jews of that place. If the prophet lived and prophesied there, his graphic descriptions of Nineveh would more easily be explained, and he would naturally be one of the Ten Tribes who were carried away thither either by Tiglath-pileser in 734, or by Sargon in 722 B. C. Ewald accepted this identification; but the tradition which associates Nahum with *Al-Kush* cannot be traced back farther than to the sixteenth century A.D. (2) *Ain-Japhata,* a town south of Babylon, where in 1165 A. D., Benjamin of Tudela was shown another traditional tomb of Nahum! (3) *El-Kauze,* a small village in North Galilee (Jerome). But Hitzig identified Capernaum in Galilee as the home of the prophet, the Arabic name *Kefr-Nahum* meaning "the city of Nahum." Compare, however, John 7:52. (4) *Elkese,* "beyond Betogabra," i. e., Beit Jibrin, 20 miles southwest of Jerusalem, in the tribe of Simeon. So, a Syriac version of *The Lives of the Prophets,* dated *ca.* 367 A. D., and erroneously ascribed to Epiphanius, bishop of Salamis; likewise, Cyril of Alexandria, and the LXX. Six miles east of *Beit Jibrin* in the *Wady es-Sur,* there is to-day a well, called by the natives *Bir el-Kaus.* Nestle favors this identification; and, indeed, this seems to be the most probable of all the identifications suggested. For at times Nahum apparently speaks from the standpoint of Judah; and, as an enthusiastic patriot, betrays his local surroundings (cf. 1:4, 15; 2:1; 3:1-7).

III. *Times.*—Nahum's date is pretty clearly indicated by 3:8-10, which treats of the fall of No-amon, i.e., Thebes in Upper Egypt, as already accomplished, and of the fall of Nineveh as shortly to take place. The former was captured by Assurbanipal in 663 B. C., and the latter by Nabopolassar in 606, or, as more recently discovered, 612 B. C. The prophet's period would accordingly fall between these two limits. Assurbanipal was exceptionally cruel. He even boasts of his violence and shameful atrocities: how he ruthlessly tore off the lips and limbs of kings, forced three captured rulers of Elam to drag his chariot through the streets, compelled a prince to wear round his neck the decapitated head of his king, and how he and his queen feasted in a garden with the head of a Chaldean monarch whom he had forced to commit suicide hanging from a tree above them. No other king even of Assyria ever boasts of such inhuman and atrocious barbarities. As he advanced toward Egypt on one of his expeditions, twenty-two kings are said to have paid him homage; upon his arrival both Memphis, the capital of Lower Egypt, and Thebes, the capital of Upper Egypt, were successfully wrested from Tirhakah and cruelly punished. The poor people of Judah and Jerusalem were spectators of all these horrors. Indeed they had beheld for generations an almost endless succession of Assyrian invasions of Palestine; Shalmanezer II in 842 B. C., Tiglath-pileser III in 734, Shalmanezer IV and Sargon II in 724-22, Sennacherib in 701, Esarhaddon in 672, and now Assurbanipal; the worst seemed yet to come. Nahum and his compatriots in Jerusalem apparently lay bound and helpless in the grasp of a cruel, tyrannical enemy (1 : 15-2 : 2). Nineveh was still at the height of her glory (3 : 16, 17). From the tone of the prophecy we may reasonably infer that the destruction of Thebes was a comparatively recent event, and that Nineveh's downfall was not yet obvious, though prophetically imminent. Hence the exact date of Nahum's ministry was probably not long after 650 B. C. If so, the prophet surely showed a daring flight of faith to declare Nineveh's certain doom when the nation as yet showed no signs of decay. Other proposed dates for Nahum's

activity, such as Hezekiah's, or Jehoiakim's, or
Zedekiah's reigns, are not so securely attested by the
events of history. Happel's attempt to explain
Nahum as a pseudepigraph of the Maccabean age is
sufficiently refuted through the previous mention of
"The Twelve Prophets" by Jesus ben Sirach in
Ecclus, 49:10, who flourished *ca.* 180 B. C. But
whatever be the prophet's correct date the Assyrian
records leave no doubt but that through all the
nation's history they were always cruel and violent
and barbaric; ever boasting of their victories, gloat-
ing that "space failed for corpses," that they "made
pyramids of human heads," and "covered pillars
with the flayed skins of their rivals!" It was upon
such a people that Nahum was commanded to pro-
nounce inexorable doom!

IV. *Nineveh.*—The city lay on the eastern side of
the Tigris, opposite the modern town of Mosul. It
was founded by Nimrod of Babylonia (Gen. 10:11),
and was especially dedicated to Istar. It was the
capital of Assyrian kings from 1100 to 880 B. C.
and again after Sennacherib became king, 705 ff.
B. C.; being regarded, as it in fact was, the chief
city of the empire. It was trebly fortified by walls
and moats, forts and towers, the walls being 7½
miles in circumference, and so broad that three
chariots could drive on their top abreast. Such was
Nineveh, the capital of the most powerful, sensual,
ferocious, and diabolically atrocious race of men that
perhaps ever existed in all the world: they were
great besiegers of men; ever crying, "Siege, siege,
siege!" But, Nahum declares, the besiegers of the
world will at last be besieged themselves (3:1 ff.).
Nahum's threats were remarkably fulfilled. Esar-

haddon was Nineveh's last king. The Medes, with
the Babylonians and the Scythians, first razed all the
surrounding fortresses (3:12), and then be-
leaguered the city. The Ninevites proclaimed a fast
of one hundred days to propitiate their gods (cf.
Jonah 3:15); nevertheless the city fell. Ktesias
describes how the last night of the besieged city was
spent in drunken orgies (1:10; 2:5), in which the
effeminate king set the example. To precipitate the
catastrophe, the Tigris overflowed, breaking
breaches in the walls, whereupon the king seeing the
fate impending, burnt himself alive in his palace
(3:15-19), and the city was, of course, subsequently
plundered of its rich spoil (2:10-14). It fell c.
611 B. C. Nineveh's destruction was made complete. All that remains to-day of the ancient city
are two great mounds, *Kouyunjik* and *Nebi Yunus*.
So complete, indeed, were Nineveh's ruins that
Xenophon scarcely recognized the site; Alexander
the Great marched by, "not knowing that a world-
empire was buried under his feet." Lucian wrote,
"Nineveh is perished, and there is no trace left where
once it was." Gibbon records that as early as A. D.
62, "the city and even the ruins of the city, had long
disappeared." The traveler Niebuhr in 1766 passed
over the site without knowing it. Only since Layard
and Botta identified the site in 1842 has the city
begun to be recognized by the modern world.

V. *Contents.*—Nahum's prophecies naturally fall
into three great divisions: (1) chap. 1, a trium-
phant paean over the impending fall of Nineveh: a
thrilling anthem! (2) chap. 2, the judgment to
be visited: the city's "den of cubs" routed; defense,
vain; (3) chap. 3, the guilt of the city: her cruelty,

and avarice, her unprincipled diplomacy, harlotry, and treachery. Nineveh, accordingly, says the prophet, will fall, totally and completely, amid the plaudits of the nations, no one being left to comfort her. The poet seems almost to revel in her destruction.

VI. *Poetic Form.*—According to poetic structure, the book may be divided into eight strophes of nearly equal length.

1. Chapter 1 : 2-6, a description of the Avenging Jehovah who will not leave crime unpunished.

2. Chapter 1 : 7-12, in order to be faithful to his own people, Jehovah must destroy Nineveh.

3. Chapter 1 : 13-2 : 2, deliverance promised to Judah, but judgment announced to Nineveh.

4. Chapter 2 : 3-8, a series of brilliant pictures descriptive of the city's capture : outside, the enemy gloriously brandishing their weapons; inside, all in confusion, chariots rattling through the streets, flashing hither and thither like lightning. But, alas! it is too late. The gates of the city have been opened, her warriors have turned in headlong flight. The queen is taken captive, and her maidens moan, beating upon their breasts.

5. Chapters 2 : 9-3 : 1, the inhabitants are terror-stricken : their "knees smite together." Woe to the bloody city, once gorged, now pillaged!

6. Chapter 3 : 2-7, fresh chariots rush against the doomed city. They are only impeded by the heaps of corpses lying about the city and in the streets. The greedy harlot lies prostrate and stripped.

7. Chapter 3 : 8-13, as No-Amon succumbed, so must Nineveh also; there is no escape.

8. Chapter 3 : 14-19, resistance will be vain. Like

devouring locusts, Nineveh's foes will come.   In fact, her king has already fallen asleep, and his people are scattered as sheep without a shepherd.   At Nineveh's collapse the nations rejoice.

As to poetic form, the book of Nahum is thus one of the finest in all the Old Testament.   No other of all the prophets, except Isaiah, can be said even to equal Nahum in boldness, ardor, or sublimity.   His descriptions are most vivid and impetuous.   "His language is strong and brilliant, his rhythm rumbles and rolls, leaps and flashes, like the horsemen and chariots he describes" (G. A. Smith).   By general consent Nahum is counted a master of Hebrew style. His supreme excellence is not his feeling but his power of description, which for fiery vigor, glowing color, dramatic impressiveness and picturesque phraseology is unsurpassed.

VII. *Message.*—The prophet really epitomizes his message in 1:7-9.   He is preëminently a prophet of one idea—the doom about to descend upon Nineveh.   Convinced that Jehovah, though slow to anger will yet take vengeance on his adversaries, he focuses the light of God's moral government upon Nineveh, and chants the death-dirge of the world's greatest oppressor.   It is the judgment of the Lord long deferred; but, judgment is sure, and it will be complete and final.   Nahum differs notably from his predecessors, as from his contemporaries, Jeremiah and Zephaniah, who were primarily interested in Israel's reformation.   Nahum says nothing about Israel's need of repentance.   Rather, the burden of his message is a certain fiery form of indignation, almost akin to animosity and revenge, and expressive of the pent-up feelings of generations of suffering

patriots which bursts forth like a flame of fire upon
Israel's national foe.   It is outraged humanity at
large which calls for vengeance.   Twice over in a
refrain which is instructive he says, "Behold, I am
against thee, saith Jehovah of hosts" (2 : 13, 3 : 5)。

VIII. *Value of His Message to Us.*—Three important lessons, implicitly taught by Nahum, stand
out as abiding: (1) the universality of God's government; (2) its retributive character; and (3) its sub-
ordination to his scheme of grace.   Such lessons can
never become obsolete.   Nahum of course had
primarily in view his own generation, but he so
framed his thoughts as to adapt them to the wants,
the guidance, and the comfort of men in all ages.
He shows plainly that Nineveh's destruction is not
an act of capricious sovereignty, but the just reward
of her iniquities.   "When once we interpret the book
eschatologically, as we ought to do, it acquires an
incomparably higher religious value than is now
generally assigned to it.   It is not the product of
mere national hatred, or even of a desire for vengeance, but a hymn to that Nemesis, at once ethical
and divine, which inexorably realizes itself in history."   (Sellin).   It is not Israel's pride that is at
stake but God's honor; and it is not even the redemption of his people that is primary, but the vindication of their God.   In other words, the great
lesson of the book is that the mills of God grind
"exceeding small"; and, that for nations as well as
for individuals, "sin when it is full-grown bringeth
forth death."   The joy of Nahum, we repeat, is not
merely the human exultation of an angry patriot
over a fallen foe, but rather the glad cry of an assured faith in the God of the fathers.   To Nahum,

Nineveh's destruction was subordinate to the saving mercy which Jehovah intended to show toward his own people and through them to the world.

"His oracle is essentially though not explicitly Messianic" (Elmslie). "The testimony of Jesus is the spirit of prophecy" (Rev. 19: 10); "Yea and all the prophets from Samuel and them that followed after . . . told of these days" (Acts 3: 24). When interpreted thus, the prophet's oracle becomes a message of consolation, which was in keeping with the prophet's name, as "Comforter." He did not hold up the Redeemer distinctly to view; it was not necessary. What he did do was to prepare them at a time when they were liable to give way to despondency. Nahum saw that the kingdom of darkness must fall before the kingdom of light breaks forth. The destruction of Nineveh, therefore, must take place before the reign of the Prince of Peace can be inaugurated. Such a message, accordingly, has a value for all time, or at least so long as there remains aught in which the spirit of Nineveh survives. Though the Book of Nahum stands in contrast to the kindlier temper and spirit of the New Testament, and naturally is not quoted by any of the writers of the New Testament, yet, imbedded in it, the Holy Spirit has implicitly predicated that every power must fall before the coming of the Kingdom of God.

IX. *Pemmican Passages.*—Certain passages are particularly precious, and unless singled out and accentuated, are liable to become overlooked in a book which, perhaps, is seldom read:

1. "Jehovah is slow to anger and great in power, and will by no means clear the guilty" (1 : 3); sug-

gesting the Italian proverb: "God does not pay on Saturday!"

2. "Jehovah is good, a stronghold in the day of trouble; and he knoweth them that take refuge in him" (1:7); the motto of "Leaves of Healing"!

3. "Behold, upon the mountains the feet of him that bringeth good tidings, that publisheth peace" (1:15)! The herald of salvation, temporal or spiritual, or both, is seen to arrive. Perhaps the original of this passage is its fuller form as found in Isaiah 52:7.

4. "She (Nineveh) is empty and void and waste, and the heart melteth, and the knees smite together" (2:10). Like other Old Testament prophets, Nahum is fond of punning! Moffat attempts to reproduce the Hebrew by translating: "She is desolate, dreary, drained—hearts are fainting, knees are shaking."

SPECIAL LITERATURE ON NAHUM

W. H. Green, "Nahum's Prophecy concerning Nineveh," *Biblical Repertory*, XXVII (1855); G. B. Gray, "The Alphabetic Poem in Nahum," *Expositor* (1898); Max Adler, "A specimen of a Comm. and Collated Text of the Targum to the Prophet Nahum," *JQR*. vii (1895); A. B. Davidson, "Nahum, Habakkuk, Zephaniah," *Cambridge Bible* (1899); Paul Ruben, "Oracle of Nahum," *Society of Bibl. Archæology* (1898; P. Haupt, *The Book of Nahum*, (1908); W. W. Cannon, "Some Notes on Nahum i-ii:3," *Expositor* (1925); C. I. Gadd, *The Fall of Nineveh*, (1923); Billerbeck and Jeremias, "Der Untergang Ninives und die Weissagschrift des Nahum von Elkosch," *Beiträge zur Assyriologie,* iii (1895) ; Bickell, in *Sitzungsberichte der Wiener Akademie der Wissenschraft,*V,(1884) ; Gunkel in *ZATW,* (1893) ; Arnold, "The Composition of Nahum 1:1-2:3," *ZATW,* (1901); Kleinert, "Nahum und der Fall Ninives," *Theol. Stud. und Krit.* (1910); Thomas Friedrich, "Ninives Ende u. die Ausgänge des Assyrischen Reiches," in *Festgaben zu Ehren Max Büdinger's* (1898) ; Staerk, *Das Assyrische Weltreich im Urteil der Propheten* (1908) ; O. Happel, *Das Buch des Propheten Nahum* (1902) ; *Ibid,* "Der Psalm des Nahum metrisch untersucht," *Theol. Quartalschrift,* ii. (1900).

CHAPTER VIII

HABAKKUK THE PHILOSOPHER

I. *Name and Personality.*—Nothing is really known of Habakkuk outside the book which bears his name. Whether, indeed, his name was originally a personal one or merely a symbolical designation is sometimes questioned (compare the name "Malachi"). It is a singular formation in any case, and may have been derived (if, indeed, it is not a loan word from the Assyrian *hambukuku,* "a species of garden plant") from the root *habhak,* meaning "to embrace"; either as a wrestler with God, or as one beloved of God, or as a comforter of his people. Luther accepted this etymology, remarking that "Habakkuk has a right name for his office. For Habakkuk means a heartener, or one who takes another to his heart and his arms, as one soothes a poor weeping child, telling it to be quiet." Like Haggai and Zechariah, he is explicitly designated "the prophet" (1:1), which may signify that he was a man of Judah and a well-known resident of Jerusalem, and, therefore, intimately acquainted with the local and political situation (1:3, 4). In any case there is ample reason for believing that he was one of the great personalities of his age; not, as Cornill suggests as possible, one of the "false prophets against whom Jeremiah urged war to the death"; but, as Stonehouse and others think, "a prominent member of the school of Isaiah"—one of Isaiah's disciples (Isa. 8:16). True, he was the "freethinker among the prophets," and in a sense the "father of Israel's religious doubt"; but he was also a man of strong faith, just the sort of man whom God customarily commissions to usher in new epochs of church history. Whether he should be identified with "the sentinel" mentioned in Isa. 21:6, sent to look for tokens of the fall of Babylon; or, as Jewish rabbis suggest, with the son of the Shunammite woman whom Elisha raised (II Kings 4:36, 37) we cannot say; but we do know that he was a philosopher, earnest and candid, and possessed of unusual originality and force, sensitive, speculative, "the suppliant" among the prophets, and the preacher of theocratic optimism.

Tradition adds many worthless details concerning him. For example, according to the story of Bel and the Dragon (vss. 33-39) he is said to have carried pottage to Daniel who had been cast a second time, by Cyrus, into the lions' den in Babylon; and according to the Preface to the same story, in the *Codex Chisianus* of the Septuagint, he belonged to the tribe of Levi, while according to the *Lives of the Prophets* he was a man of the tribe of Simeon, who, when Nebuchadnezzar advanced to take Jerusalem, fled to Ostrakine, twenty-six miles west of El-'Arish on the Egyptian coast, but returned to his own land where he died and was buried two years before the return of the Jews from Babylon in 536 B. C. Eusebius in his *Onomasticon* adds that in his day his tomb was shown at both Gibeah and Keilah!

II. *Aim.*—The sole aim of the prophet was to

foretell the coming downfall of the Chaldeans and thereby to give encouragement to Judah in time of crisis. Very appropriately the book opens with a title descriptive of its character, "the burden which Habakkuk the prophet did see" (1 : 1). The word "burden" prepares the reader to expect a "solemn utterance," presumably a threatening judgment or judicial sentence against some foreign foe. Other prophets usually denounced the sins of their own people; it was for Habakkuk to emphasize the violence and excess of Judah's threatening oppressors, the Chaldeans.

III. *Date.*—The date of Habakkuk's prophecies turns on the identification of the Chaldeans as the tyrants of his times, more exactly the specific time when they set out upon their career of conquest (1 : 6); for there is no indication in the book that they had as yet interfered directly with the affairs of Judah. Many authorities agree on the year 604-603 B. C. Nineveh had fallen in 606, or possibly as early as 612 B. C. Nebuchadnezzar had just fairly started on his celebrated career of conquest in Western Asia. At Carchemish he defeated Pharaoh-necho of Egypt in 605. This last victory was the turning point in the history of that age. Egypt, which had sorely beset Judah between 608 and 605, was now humbled by the Chaldean conquerors. The times were anxious ones for Judah. Josiah's reformation in 621 had proven superficial. Destruction and violence were being perpetrated by the Chaldeans on the nations generally (1 : 5, 10, 13; 2 : 5, 6). Judah had not yet actually been invaded, but Lebanon had already begun to suffer (2 : 14), and the nearer and nearer approach of the enemy

was having a bad effect on the life of Judah (1:4).
All these considerations taken together point to a
date shortly after the battle of Carchemish, or about
603 B. C. Jewish tradition, however, assigns the
book to the reign of Manasseh; Betteridge, to 701
B. C.; Budde and Cornill, to *ca.* 615; v. Orelli, to
"before 605"; Duhm, to 334-331; Happel, to the
reign of Antiochus IV, *ca.* 170. But the date to be
preferred is 603. The first temple is presumably
still standing (2:20).

IV. *Analysis and Contents.*—The book opens
with a dialogue between Jehovah and the prophet,
then records certain woes against the violent oppressor of mankind, and closes with a beautiful poem
of confidence that God will deliver his people. It
may be easily separated into six distinct and characteristic divisions:

1. *The prophet's complaint* (1:2-4).—He begins
with a wail of despair, "O Jehovah, how long shall
I cry and thou wilt not hear?" His fundamental
difficulty is why Jehovah permits evil. He seriously
deprecates the divine indifference to wrongdoing, for
violence and injustice reign on every side, "the
Torah is slacked and justice doth never go forth"
(vs. 4). He faces a real problem. The Torah is
paralyzed. He does not complain, however, *against*
God, but *to* God. He does not ask what the meaning of it all is, he knows it is "for judgment" and
"for correction" (1:12); nor does he directly question why evil should be allowed to triumph, but he
does ask what will be the issue. "How long?"
Wickedness beleaguers the righteous and thwarts
their purpose; why, therefore, does Jehovah not
intervene?

But the question naturally arises, What were the wrongs which the prophet decries in these verses? Are they domestic, i.e., those committed by Hebrews against Hebrews in Judah? Or are they the direful effects of an approaching and threatening foe like the Chaldeans from without? Opinions differ, but in view of vs. 13 it is more natural to think of the latter. The anticipated invasion of the Chaldeans was producing friction and strife, and discord, and lawlessness, and anarchy in Judah; and Habakkuk accordingly cries out.

2. *Jehovah's response* (1:5-11).—He says, "I am working a work in your days" (vs. 5), using a drastic method—raising up the Chaldeans—to scourge his own people. These verses contain a most graphic description of the character and conquests of the Chaldeans, that bitter and hasty nation, dispossessing the inhabitants of the whole earth, terrible and dreadful, who gather captives as the sand, scoff at kings, capture strongholds, take cities and, though unspeakably cruel and guilty, dare to deify their own might!

3. *The prophet's moral problem* (1:12-2:1).— Jehovah's answer, while strengthening the prophet's faith, creates a new and more serious moral problem. God's method confuses him. Why should Jehovah, even though he has raised up the Chaldeans "for judgment" and "for correction" (vs. 12), use treacherous foes who are dragging men more righteous than themselves (vs. 13) into their net like fishes, and who fail to see in their successes the hand of God? In other words, how can God reconcile the cruelty of the Chaldeans with his own purity and holiness (vs. 13)? The tyrant has out-

raged humanity. Is there no divine providence?
How can God use such a cruel and barbarous nation
to execute judgment on his own chosen people? Are
they continually to destroy the nations and spare
not? Surely such judgment is only temporary (vs.
17). Habakkuk's problem penetrates the moral,
meaning of Israel's experience and history. It is
the problem of the strength of the wicked versus the
humiliation of the just. He finds the solution to his
enigma only when he climbs the watchtower of faith;
for, though he sees the world in ruins all about him,
he is soon brought back to a firm belief in the providence of God (2:1).

4. *Jehovah's final reply* (2:2-4).—Standing upon
his watchtower, Habakkuk has not long to wait
for Jehovah's reply. He receives a vision and is
bidden to inscribe it on tablets so plainly "that he
may run that readeth it," for it contains a message
the fulfilment of which lies in the future. So he
exhorts, "though it tarry, wait for it; because it will
surely come, it will not delay" (vs. 3). The imagery
seems to be that of a city intrenched against the invasion of a foe. The prophet feels he has a post to
hold, a rampart to guard. From this lofty vantage
ground he at length finds the key to his long-standing
and troublesome riddle, and is inspired by it to
enunciate the great moral principle of true religion,
namely, that pride and tyranny cannot from the
nature of them, last, but that the righteous, if only
steadfast, shall survive: "Behold his soul is puffed
up, it is not upright in him; but the righteous shall
live by his faith" (2:4). In other words, the future
belongs to the righteous; whereas, those whose souls
are "puffed up" and arrogant have no future! The

Chaldeans are self-centered, and are therefore doomed; the righteous are God-centered and are therefore permanent.

5. *A series of five woes* (2:5-20).—In a fivefold series of anathemas the vanquished and enslaved nations lift their voices in condemnation of the Chaldean oppressors (vs. 5). Habakkuk's indictments remind one of those brought by Nahum against Nineveh. The prophet believes that the smiter shall himself be smitten; that tyranny is suicide; that the Chaldeans are criminals; and that injustice inherently and necessarily tends to decay. Speaking for the desolated nations, therefore, he heaps upon them a fivefold taunting and sarcastic invective.

(1) Woe to him who ambitiously lusts for new conquests in order to gain plunder; such a plunderer shall himself be plundered; as he has spoiled, so shall he be spoiled (vss. 6-8).

(2) Woe to him who coveteously thinks only of individual gain and self-aggrandizement, selfishly seeking only to secure his own resources and guard himself against misfortune; such a policy is suicidal and its advocate in due time forfeits his own soul (vss. 9-11).

(3) Woe to him who unscrupulously oppresses others; for cities built by cruelty and violence shall be destroyed (vss. 12-14).

(4) Woe to him who barbarously reduces a vanquished people to utter helplessness in order to gloat over their subject condition; for with what measure he metes it shall be measured unto him again (vss. 15-17).

(5) Woe to him who foolishly resorts to dumb

idols for instruction; for idolatry is silly and irrational and a molten image is only a teacher of lies (vss. 18-20). Jehovah reigns!

6. *An ode or rhapsody* (chap. 3).—The third chapter of Habakkuk is one of the most beautiful anthems of praise in the Old Testament. It is bold in conception, sublime in thought, majestic in diction, and pure in rhetoric. Ewald speaks of it as "Habakkuk's Pindaric Ode." It falls naturally into three divisions:

(1) A prayer, beseeching Jehovah to renew his work of deliverance as of old, now, "in the midst of the years" (vs. 2).

(2) A theophany; Jehovah comes from Teman and Paran in a thundercloud (vss. 3-15; cf. Deut. 33:2; Judg. 5:4).

(3) The effect of Jehovah's wonderful appearance upon the prophet, at first producing fear and suspense, but afterward calm and joyous confidence (vss. 16-19).

This poem, like chaps. 1-2, was evidently written at a time of national crisis, when the land was threatened by invasion (3:16). Its sentiment is in wonderful accord with that of Habakkuk's own undisputed prophecies (chaps. 1-2): in the latter he begins with mystery and interrogation (1:2); in the song he concludes with certainty and affirmation (3:19). The same lofty tone and temper pervade them both. Their purpose is apparently the same: the song supplements the prophet's message, that of each being to encourage and keep alive within the nation a spirit of hope and trust in God. Accordingly, he represents Jehovah as coming in a storm-cloud from his mountain home in the desert to rescue his people from their foes. The theophany is solely for Israel's deliverance and salvation (vs. 13). His argument is that he who so wonderfully delivered his people in their youth will not forsake them "in the midst of the years." Jehovah having worked for Israel's redemption in the days of Moses and the Judges will do so again in the present crisis. He, therefore, expects a new *parousia* of Jehovah—a self-revelation of his person, and a sudden unveiling of his glory—for salvation (vs. 13). And in this expectation and faith he concludes, with absolute and unbounded confidence in God, emphatically affirming that though all visible signs of his love should fail and he should be reduced to poverty and penury he will yet rejoice in the God of his salvation (vss. 17, 18). Ps. 77 : 15-20 shows traces of the influence of the poem.

'Tis true the psalm bears marks of having once belonged to a songbook of the Jewish community. The word "selah," which announces a paragraph division, occurs thrice (vss. 3, 9, 13). The psalm possesses a superscription which designates both the author and the character of the poem (vs. 1) as customarily in the Psalter; but the accompanying phrase "set to Shigionoth," which many regard as a musical direction, is to be taken preferably, as by Thirtle, to mean "for adversity." The true musical direction stands as a subscription: "For the Chief Musician," as in fifty-four psalms, accompanied by the additional words "on my stringed instruments." But because such musical and kindred annotations have no parallels in other prophetical books, we do not need to conclude that Habakkuk did not compose

the poem; for chaps. 1-2 are proof enough surely
that the prophet was a real poet!

V. *Permanent Teaching.*—Habakkuk was content
to enunciate one single great truth, but one so great
that it has since become not only the motto of
Judaism but also of evangelical Christianity—the
doctrine of justification by faith (2:4). It was not
Luther, nor Augustine, nor even Paul who first
taught this great principle, but Habakkuk, doing so
on the eve of the Chaldean invasion of Judah. It
may be resolved into several component elements.

1. *The fact of divine discipline.*—The constant
riddle of the Old Testament is "not the survival of
the fittest but the suffering of the best." In Job it
was the suffering of an individual; in Habakkuk, that
of a nation.

2. *The fact that evil is self-destructive.*—With
singular arrogance the Chaldeans were blind to the
fact that they were but the rod of Jehovah's vengeance. Jeremiah and Habakkuk were contemporaries: Jeremiah taught that wickedness in God's
own people is doomed; Habakkuk, that wickedness
in the Chaldeans, also, is doomed. Tyranny always
carries within it the seeds of its own destruction.

3. *The fact that faith is the condition of life.*—
"The righteous shall live by his faith." This is the
great teaching of Habakkuk. In it the prophet made
a most original and very significant contribution to
the world's theology. "Faith" to the prophet meant
more than simple trust. The form is a feminine abstract, *'emunah,* and conveys, as the use of the word
elsewhere in the Old Testament warrants (cf. Exod.
17:12; Isa. 33:6; II Kings 22:7; I Chron. 9:22,
26; Prov. 12:17), the idea of the temper which

trust produces, namely, faithfulness, steadfastness, firmness, persistency, endurance, patience, even loyalty. And "life" to Habakkuk meant not mere national prosperity, but moral security, even in the midst of calamity. In other words, a living faith determines destiny: abiding in life and surviving in judgment. Habakkuk as a philosopher traveled all the way from doubt to a higher faith. This passage of Habakkuk (2:4) is quoted three times in the New Testament (Rom. 1:17; Gal. 3:11; Heb. 10:38).

Incidentally, also, Habakkuk teaches two other important lessons:

1. *The vanity of violence.*—"O Jehovah, thou hast ordained him for judgment; and thou, O Rock, hast established him for correction" (1:12); and,

2. *Courage in time of crisis* (3:17-19).—Habakkuk implicitly exhorts his readers to be courageous and happy. Mass begins with the words *Sursum corda,* "Up with your hearts." So Habakkuk, to the soul cut off from all outward possessions, gives the exhortation to be courageous and happy still in God alone, as the object of his confidence. This was apparently native to him and therefore natural, for he possessed an ever joyous confidence that Jehovah would bring salvation.

SPECIAL LITERATURE ON HABAKKUK

G. G. V. Stonehouse, *The Book of Habakkuk* (1911); A. B. Davidson, "The Books of Nahum, Habakkuk, and Zephaniah," *Cambridge Bible* (1896); W. B. Stevenson, "The Interpretation of Habakkuk," *Expositor* (1902); F. T. Kelly, "The

Strophic Structure of Habakkuk," *Amer. Journal of Semitic Langs. and Literatures* (1902); W. R. Betteridge, *Amer. Journal of Theology* (1903); T. K. Cheyne, *Critica Biblica* (1904); *Ibid, Jewish Quarterly Review* (1908); K. Budde, *Expositor* (1895); F. Delitzsch, *Der Prophet Habakkuk* (1893); J. von Gumpach, *Der Prophet Habakuk* (1860); Sinker, *The Psalm of Habakkuk* (1890); D. Happel, *Das Buch des Propheten Habackuk* (1900); B. Duhm, *Das Buch Habakuk* (1906); F. Nicolardot, *La Composition du livre d'Habacuc* (1908); Katwijk, *Die Prophetie van Habakuk* (1912); J. W. Rothstein, *Theologische Studien und Kritiken* (1894); Caspari, "Die Chaldäer bei Habaquq," *Neue kirkliche Zeitschrift* (1907); F. E. Peiser, *Der Prophet Habakuk* (1903).

CHAPTER IX

ZEPHANIAH THE ORATOR

I. *Name and Genealogy.*—Two other Zephaniahs, besides the prophet, are mentioned in the Old
Testament: one, a Kohathite, ancestor of Heman the
singer (I Chron. 6:36); the other, a pro-Egyptian
priest, contemporaneous with Jeremiah (II Kings
25:18; Jer. 21:1; 37:3). Etymologically the
name means "He whom Jehovah has hidden or pro-
tected" (cf. Ps. 27:5); a significance which especially fits the prophet's message. His personality,
in fact, is imbedded in his message. As in the
cases of Isaiah, Jeremiah, Joel, and Zechariah,
Zephaniah's pedigree is given (1:1); with very
unusual detail, however, as the great-great-grandson
of Hezekiah, who presumably is to be identified with
Hezekiah, the famous king of Judah, otherwise there
would be no rational grounds for tracing his
genealogy four generations back. That Zephaniah
really did belong to a side line of the royal family is
chronologically possible, as Manasseh the son of
Hezekiah was forty-five years old when his son
Amon was born (II Kings 21:1, 19). By that time
Manasseh's brother, Amariah, might easily have had
a grandson (Cushi), hence Zephaniah may have been
quite as old as Josiah. If, then, Zephaniah was of
royal blood, his strictures on the princes and other

potentates of Jerusalem in 1 : 8, 9, become more interesting and far more pertinent! He evidently
lived in Jerusalem, as his familiarity with "the fish
gate" and "Maktesh," (probably some particular
business quarter of the city, 1 : 10, 11), would indicate, especially his reference to "this place" in 1 : 4.

II. *Period and Date*.—The title declares that
Zephaniah prophesied "in the days of Josiah" (639-
608 B. C.), and with this statement the tenor of the
book entirely agrees. As Elmslie observes, "There
is nothing in the book to justify the faintest sus-
picion that it does not belong to this period." Yet
though he condemns his people for their idolatry and
corruption, violence and injustice, the full truth is
that he "tears himself loose from history altogether," because the universal character of his message excluded concrete treatment of historical events.
It cannot be said in fact that Zephaniah spoke out of
some particular panic, or danger, such as that of the
Scythian invasion which descended on Palestine
about this time, 627 B. C. (Herodotus i. 104 ff.),
though this is, of course, possible. Zephaniah rather
shows a studied indefiniteness concerning all passing
events.

Whether, however, he prophesied before the discovery of the Book of the Law in the eighteenth
year of Josiah's reign, 621 B. C. (II Kings 22 : 8),
as most modern scholars agree, or after this epoch-
making event, as Delitzsch, Kleinert, and Schulz
argue, will depend largely upon our interpretation
of the following references: (1) "the remnant of
Baal" (1 : 4), which seems to place him after at least
Josiah's twelfth year when he began to reform (II
Chron. 34 : 3); compare the LXX, however which

reads "name" instead of "remnant," in vs. 4.   (2)
"the king's sons" (1:8). Would the young king in
his early twenties already have "sons"? (II Kings
21:1, 3).   But, again, the LXX reads "the king's
house," which may have been meant to include all
the members of the royal family.   (3) The
prophet's threat of overthrow and desolation on
Nineveh (2:13-15) has none of the rancour which
seems to characterize Nahum; hence, perhaps
Zephaniah was a little earlier than Nahum.   (4)
"They have done violence to the law" (3:4). This
passage might seem to point to a time after the
great reformation of Josiah in 621 B. C.; but
Jeremiah alludes to "the priests" and "the law" in
the very beginning of his ministry (Jer. 2:8), and
Jeremiah and Zephaniah were close contemporaries,
having begun to preach probably about the same
year, 626 B. C.   Hence we may conclude that
Zephaniah prophesied between Josiah's twelfth and
eighteenth years, or about 625 B. C.

III. *Contents.*—Three distinct stages, or phases,
can be traced in Zephaniah's treatment of his one
great theme, the coming day of Jehovah:

1. Threatening and judgment (chap. 1); announcing with denunciation and menace the day of
Jehovah's wrath, which would embrace the entire
earth, but which was directed particularly against
the idolators and apostates in Judah and Jerusalem.

2. Warnings and admonitions (chap. 2), to the
nations: Philistia, Moab, Ammon, Ethiopia, and
Assyria; followed by an earnest appeal to Jerusalem
to repent, in order to escape the doom destined to
fall on wilful sinners (3:1-7).

3. Encouragement and promise (3:8-20); of

salvation to those who repent, especially to "the remnant of Israel," who shall rejoice in world-wide fame as the redeemed of Jehovah, dwelling forever in his presence.

IV. *Theme.*—The great and only theme of Zephaniah is the coming "day of Jehovah," when the Lord would reveal himself in his fulness to the whole world, judging evil doers, and fulfilling his great purposes of redemption among men. But judgment is not regarded by Zephaniah as an end in itself; it is rather a means of making Jehovah known to the world and the ushering in of his kingdom of salvation. His theme, accordingly, is little less than "the consummation of the world's history."

To Zephaniah, the day of Jehovah meant not so much a great day of assize, as a day of battle; an apocalyptic world-conflict which was on the way. The people were "settled on their lees," i. e., they were corrupt and selfish, and their lives were stagnated into a practical indifferentism which was little better than atheism. Hence, slaughter and destruction awaited them. Jehovah's guests are already invited to the great sacrifice. Everything will be burned up. "That day is a day of wrath" (1 : 15); this text having furnished the basis of the most striking of medieval hymns: *Dies Irae, Dies Illa,* "Day of wrath! O day of mourning." For Zephaniah's note of doom for the nations seems to have reverberated through the ages till it fell upon the ears of the Franciscan Thomas of Celano, a devout Italian monk of the thirteenth century, and, as a result, in a poem of nineteen verses, he has given to the world an acknowledged masterpiece, so awful in its grandeur and so intense in its earnestness and pathos that we hear in it, as it were, "the final crash of the universe!" Zephaniah's message must have helped forward the reformation of King Josiah; for, he directed his blows against religious syncretism—a mixture of Baal, Milcom, and star worship—and exhorted his people to seek meekness and righteousness, promising that, if they did, all would be well. It is unfair to say that his message is "wholly negative and destructive." That statement is true only when the promissory portions are detached by an illogical and unscientific criticism.

V. *Value.*—The Book of Zephaniah, though small, is nevertheless, valuable. By many it is undervalued, and by most of us passed by as comparatively barren of pulpit texts; on the contrary, it is of abiding value, and as a book should not be estimated by its size. Here are some of its permanent teachings:

1. *The constant necessity of warning* (1:14-16). —Zephaniah sets all modern prophets an example of how men should be confronted with the stern realities of the moral world.

2. *The profoundly earnest moral tone which pervades the entire book.*—Zephaniah is deeply sensitive of the sins of his people, and of the moral need which impels Jehovah to visit them with discipline and judgment. His gospel is "simple and austere." A moral sifting is necessary (3:7-13).

3. *The spiritual nature of God's kingdom* (3:14-20).—This section is one of the earliest of Old Testament apocalypses; it is "the finest thing in the book," and contains two wonderful promises: (a) "Jehovah is in the midst of thee" (vss. 15, 17); and (b) "I will make of you a name and a praise

among all peoples" (v. 20). For after tribulation comes glorification. Judah's captivity will be reversed; all turns out well. She shall be saved, "yet so as by fire." The remnant of Jehovah shall enjoy "a modest golden age." While there is no explicit reference to a personal Messiah in Zephaniah's prophecies, yet we may well believe that whatever the prophet himself saw in this apocalyptic vision, his words look forward to the Great Deliverance wrought by Christ. Most remarkable is the fact that his conception of the heavenly kingdom includes all mankind.

VI. *Style.*—Zephaniah's style is direct and forceful, and, therefore, in keeping with the imperative character of his message. What he lacks in grace and charm he in some measure makes up in vigor and clarity of speech. "No prophet has made the picture of the day of Jehovah more real." The thunder of his *Dies Irae,* which the whole musical world now sings as a requiem, rolls in powerful dirge-like meter of drastic vividness, so musical and so beautiful that no translator can render it without great loss into another language. Budde was the first to recognize that the bulk of the book was written in this *kinah,* or elegiac meter. For an announcement of chastisement and affliction, this kind of poetry, in lines of 3+2 beats each, is the most suitable measure. Excepting 2:8-11 and 3:16-20, the whole book is practically of this form. A passage of exquisite beauty is 3:11-13.

Zephaniah is perhaps less original than most of the other prophets. He shows affinity with his predecessors, especially with the style of Isaiah; yet the stream of his discourse flows along smoothly and gravely. His repetitions of words and phrases only enhance his emphasis. Occasionally, he puns, e.g., in 2:4, *Azzah, azubah; Ekron, teaker:* "Gaza shall be forgotten, and Ekron shall be uncrowned." Certain of his epigrams are very striking: e. g., "I will search Jerusalem with lamps," and "I will punish the men that are settled on their lees," 1:12; "They shall walk like blind men," 1:17; "He hath consecrated his guests, 1:7; "O nation that hath no shame," 2:1, and, "Only fear thou me; receive correction," 3:7. It has been said: "If any one desires to see the utterances of the prophets in brief space, let him read through this brief Book of Zephaniah." "What is new in Zephaniah is especially the extended survey of all lands and nations and the general review of the spiritual affairs of the whole earth" (Ewald).

SPECIAL LITERATURE ON ZEPHANIAH

Beside the *Commentaries* covering the whole Twelve, also articles on "Zephaniah" in *Dictionaries* and *Encyclopædias,* and *Introductions* by Driver, Cornill, Mackay, McFadyen, Elmslie (in *Book by Book*), Moore, Gray, Raven, Wright, Bennett, Sellin, and others; the following *Monographs,* and special *Articles* on Zephaniah, his poetry, etc., should be consulted: J. T. Beck, *Erklärung der Propheten Nahum und Zephanja* (1899); E. Besson, *Introduction au Prophète Sophonie* (1910); J. Bachmann, "Zur Textkritik des Propheten Zephanja," *Stud. u. Krit.* (1894); K. Budde, *Stud. u. Krit.* (1893); C. H. Cornill, "Die Prophetie Zephaniahs," *Stud. u. Krit.* (1916); D. H. Müller, *Wiener Zeitschrift für die Kunde des Morgenlandes* (1905).

CHAPTER X

HAGGAI THE PROPHET OF TEMPLE BUILDING

I. *Personal History.*—Little is known of Haggai beyond the fact that he was the first prophet of the newly established Jewish colony which returned to Jerusalem from Babylon in 536 B.C. Both in his own book and in Ezra 5 : 1, he is introduced simply as "Haggai the prophet." From Hag. 2 : 3 Ewald inferred that he was an old man when he prophesied, probably between seventy and eighty years of age. In any case he seems to have been the senior of Zechariah, for Haggai, when their names occur together, is always spoken of first, Ezra 5 : 1; 6 : 14. One ancient tradition, indeed, declares that he was born in Jerusalem, carried into captivity by Nebuchadnezzar, and allowed by Cyrus to return to the Holy City. On the other hand, Epiphanius, in his *Vitae prophetarum,* states that he came up from Babylon while still young.

The Greek, Latin, and Syriac Versions associate his name with Zechariah's at the head of certain psalms as their possible author: e. g., Ps. 111 in the Vulgate; Pss. 125, 126 in the Peshitto; Ps. 137 in the Septuagint; Pss. 146-148 in both the Septuagint and Peshitto; and Ps. 145 in the Septuagint, Peshitto, and Vulgate. But it is thought by some to be more probable that these psalms were merely introduced into the temple service on the recommendation of these prophets who were men of great faith, cf. Hag. 2 : 2-9. Haggai, especially, was a prophet whose faith was akin to assurance; he was sure of his message, 1 : 13. It is even possible that he was also a priest, 2 : 10-19. Jewish tradition makes him a member of the Great Synagogue.

His name in Hebrew is from a root descriptive of excited or rapid movement such as dancing; from which it may be inferred that he was probably born on some festal day; compare the Roman name "Festus." Hebrew proper names were sometimes formed in this manner: for example, Barzillai, "a man of iron," from *barzel*, "iron." On the other hand, it is possible that the name "Haggai" may be a contraction of *Haggiah*, meaning "festival of Jehovah," I Chron. 6 : 30; as "Mattenai" is a contraction of *Mattaniah*, Ezra 10 : 26, 33. Or his name may be an abbreviation of *Hagariah*, "Jehovah girdeth"; as "Zacchaeus" is of Zechariah.

II. *His Work.*—The rebuilding of the temple is the center of interest around which all that Haggai preached revolves. For it was his supreme mission to arouse the Jews of Jerusalem to rise up and rebuild the temple of Solomon, which Nebuchadnezzar had destroyed in 586 B. C. No prophet ever preached more directly or earnestly to his own contemporaries, and no prophet was ever more successful. His junior colleague, Zechariah, was likewise called to assist in the same great enterprise; the difference between them being that Haggai preached during a short period of critical stress, whereas

Zechariah added to his visions of temple-building spiritual prophecies of edification for all time.

III. *His Period and Circumstances.*—All of Haggai's prophecies (like many of Ezekiel's) are dated as falling "in the second year of Darius," which is known to be 520 B. C., 1 : 1, 15 ; 2 : 10. The book of Ezra, however, furnishes most of the details of the history of his period and work, Ezra 1 : 1-4 : 5 ; 4 : 24-6 : 15. It tells us how a second exodus, so to speak, took place in 536 B.C., when Cyrus, king of Persia, gave the Jews permission to return to Jerusalem, 1 : 1-4 ; and how 42,360 under the leadership of Zerubbabel, the civil head of the community, and Joshua, the ecclesiastical, returned to the Holy Land, and settled in Jerusalem, and in the neighboring towns of Bethlehem, Bethel, Anathoth, Gibeon, and elsewhere, chap. 2. The book of Ezra also tells us how Cyrus' permission to rebuild the temple remained a dead letter for years, 4 : 1 ff. For, though the Jewish colonists had returned from Babylon eager and enthusiastic to reestablish the worship of their sanctuary, and had set up the altar of burnt-offering upon its old site, 3 : 2, 3, and had even laid the foundations of the temple itself, 3 : 8-10, yet we know that they were compelled to desist from completing it because of the jealousy of the semi-pagan, half-caste, Samaritans (descendants of the colonists introduced into Samaria by Sargon in 722 B. C., II Kings 17 : 24-41) whose offer to co-operate in the reconstruction of the sacred edifice they had peremptorily refused, 4 : 1-5, 24 ; cf. 5 : 16. Consequently for sixteen years the work of rebuilding stood still ; apathy supplanting enthusiasm, and sordid money-making absorbing

their chief interests.   Indeed, it seems that in course
of time the people began almost to welcome opposition to their task because it furnished them an opportunity to construct "ceiled houses" for themselves, Hag. 1 : 4.   But lean years followed, due, as
Haggai reminds them, to Jehovah's displeasure,
1 : 1-11.

Professor W. H. Kosters of Leiden, on the other
hand, attempted to show, several years ago, that
there was no return of the Jews from captivity under
Cyrus, and that Haggai and Zechariah, who never
allude to it, but rather regard Israel's return as still
future, cf. Zech. 2 : 6, 7, preached to the Jewish
remnant who remained in Jerusalem after Nebuchadnezzar had carried away the flower of the
nation in 586 B. C.   But, in spite of the plausibility
of Kosters' theory, the account contained in Ezra,
chaps. 1-4, which describes the return of 42,360
under Zerubbabel and Joshua, warrants serious and
hearty credence.   Kosters has few disciples.

With the accession of Darius, the son of
Hystaspis, however, a new era in the history of the
new colony was inaugurated.   Politically it was a
critical period.   In the year 521 B. C. Darius,
having removed the usurper Pseudo-Smerdis, who
had held the throne for seven months, began to reign
over the ill-compacted Persian Empire.   His work
was necessarily that of political organization.   His
predecessors, Cyrus and Cambyses, had been occupied chiefly with wars of conquest, and, therefore,
found little opportunity to consolidate the various
tribes who were nominally subject to the Persian
government.   Many of these tribes were restless
and rebellious.   Insurrections broke out all over the

empire on the accession of Darius, Hag. 2 : 7, 22;
the provinces of Susiana, Media, Assyria, Armenia,
and Parthia, twenty-three in all, rebelled, giving the
king serious trouble; cf. the famous Behistun Inscription of Darius. Altogether Darius fought
nineteen battles in subduing recalcitrant tribes.
Meanwhile the Persian Empire was shaken to its
foundations, especially the year during a part of
which Haggai preached, 520 B.C. This fact ac-
counts for the prophet's repeated allusions to Jehovah's "shaking" the nations, Hag. 2 : 6, 7, 21, 22.
He seems to regard the "shaking" of the nations as
the precursor of the messianic age, and the rebuilding of the Temple as the necessary preparation for
the reception of the Divine King.

IV. *Analysis.*—Haggai's prophecies, being dated,
are therefore easily analyzed:

1. Chapter 1 : 1-11, delivered on the first day of
the sixth month (September); containing the
prophet's reproaches because of the people's indifference to Jehovah's house, and pillorying them for it;
warning them also that their apathy toward temple-
building had caused God to withhold from them the
produce of the field, 1 : 10; cf. 2 : 16, and exhorting
them to "consider" their ways, 1 : 5, 7. The effect
of this open but appealing remonstrance was that
twenty-four days later the people began to work,
1 : 14-15.

2. Chapter 2 : 1-19, delivered on the twenty-first
day of the seventh month (October); containing a
note of real encouragement to those whose ambitions
to build a temple, worthy of comparison with that
constructed aforetime by Solomon, were likely to be
disappointed. On the contrary, the prophet assures

them that Jehovah will "shake" the nations and that "the precious things of all nations shall come" to beautify and glorify the new structure, Hag. 2 : 7, 8; cf. Hebs. 12 : 26-28.

3. Chapter 2 : 10-19, delivered on the twenty-fourth day of the ninth month (December), exactly three months after the work of building had been resumed, containing, like the first discourse, a rebuke to the people because of their inertia, and an assurance that their neglect of the temple had tainted their whole moral life. This discourse in part is couched in the form of a parable, vss. 11-14, by means of which he shows them how a single taint of guilt vitiates everything they do. On the other hand, if they will push forward the work of temple reconstruction, Jehovah will again bless them and fruitful seasons will follow their renewed zeal, 2 : 19; Zech. 8 : 9-12.

4. Chapter 2 : 20-23, delivered on the same date as the third discourse; announcing that in the approaching catastrophe when "the throne of the kingdoms" will be overthrown, Zerubbabel shall be established as the representative of the Davidic dynasty, the object of Israel's patriotic hope, God's honored and trusted vice-gerent—yea, the precious "signet" on Jehovah's hand, cf. Jer. 22 : 24.

V. *Permanent Lessons.*—Haggai's message of only thirty-eight verses (which of course are but a brief epitome of the prophet's more formidable discourses) gave effective impetus to the cause of temple-building, as witnessed to by Ezra, chapters 5 : 1; 6 : 14. The result of his preaching was a great victory. For, to persuade a whole people to make pecuniary sacrifices, and to postpone their own private interests for the sake of a public sanctuary, was no easy task. But Haggai did it, and by succeeding became the true founder of post-exilic Judaism; his work being preparatory to that of Ezra and Nehemiah. Among the lessons from Haggai of permanent value are the following:

1. *The Divine origin of all successful preaching.* —The most striking sentence in all Haggai's writings is that found in 1:13, "Then spake Haggai Jehovah's messenger, in Jehovah's message to the people." Repeatedly the prophet tells us that "the word of Jehovah came" unto him, 2:1, 10, 20; very often also he uses the expression, "Thus saith Jehovah of hosts," 1:2, 5, 6, 7; 2:11; cf. 1:9; 2:7, 9, 23; also, 2:4, 14, 17. And he frequently emphasizes Jehovah's presence with the nation, "For I am with you," 1:13; 2:4; promising for Jehovah, ten times over, that he will do various things in Israel's behalf, "I will be glorified," "I will give peace," "I will overthrow the thrones of kingdoms," etc. It is indeed on the ground of such absolute conviction, that Haggai ventures to exhort his people to "consider their ways," 1:5, 7; cf. 2:15, 18.

2. *The contagious character of the sin of procrastination.*—By a somewhat unusual parable contained in 2:10-19, he teaches that while holiness is not contagious, unholiness is. "The faint aroma of sanctity coming from their altar sacrifices, was too feeble to pervade the secular atmosphere of their life." On the other hand, their long sixteen-year postponement of rebuilding God's house had rendered them unclean in the Divine sight, and had brought them only blasting and mildew and hail, instead of bountiful harvests, 2:15, 16. He argues,

that while a healthy man cannot give his health to another by touching him, a sick man may easily spread contagion to those about him. In other words, he tells them there is a "dead thing" among them, namely, the fact that Jehovah's house lieth waste, 1 : 9; 2 : 13, 14, and that by treating it indifferently they have become unclean and contaminated.

3. *The church the religious center of the world.*—He says, "I will shake all nations: and the precious things of all nations shall come: and I will fill this house with glory, saith Jehovah of hosts. The silver is mine, and the gold is mine, saith Jehovah of hosts," 2 : 7, 8; cf. Isa. 2 : 2-4. Thus, the prophet attaches almost sacramental significance to the temple. Compare Ezekiel, chaps. 40-48. Such a conception can be adequately fulfilled, of course, only in a spiritual sense; and thus it is interpreted in Heb. 12 : 26-28. The rendering of the phrase in the A. V. of 2 : 7 as "the desire of all nations," instead of "the precious things of all nations," as in the American R. V., is, as one has called it, "an exquisite mistranslation," due, of course, to Jerome's use of the Latin word "Desideratus," to express the original. The Hebrew verb employed in connection with it is a plural, which intimates that the phrase "the precious things of all nations" probably includes a plethora of good things, coveted by all nations, such as "rest," which Buddha longed to find, and "light" for which Zoroaster strove, and "power," of which the Romans were so proud, and "beauty," which the Greeks so ardently cultivated.

4. *Messianic royalty and kingship.*—Haggai's concluding word of promise is that Jehovah will take

Zerubbabel his "servant" and make him "as a signet," whom he has "chosen," 2:23. Wellhausen and a few others interpret these words concerning Zerubbabel to mean that Zerubbabel is here designated as the expected Messiah promised by the former prophets; but it is probably quite enough to think that the prophet points to him as merely the object of the nation's patriotic hopes; that in the "shaking" of the nations, he, Zerubbabel, the grandson of Jehoiachin, who had been degraded from the kingly office, Jer. 22:24, would continue to be the honored and trusted vice-gerent of Jehovah, and would thus link up the political hope of the post-exilic congregation to the royal line of Judah's messianic predictions. Isaiah speaks of Cyrus in similar terms without any specific messianic implications, Isa. 44:28; 45:1. Nevertheless, in the prominence Haggai thus gives to the temple and Zerubbabel, we have a harbinger of the greater glory of the second temple through Jesus Christ.

VI. *Style.*—While Haggai's style is less poetical than that of his predecessors, yet it is hardly fair to speak of him as "crabbed," "threadbare," and "poverty-stricken" in vocabulary; for his style is admirably suited to his message and the end he had in view. His style, though plain and unadorned, is telling; simple and prosaic, sometimes even ponderous, but at the same time, stern and forceful; his short, sharp sentences being exactly what the occasion required to reform, to correct, and to restore. While the mantle of prophecy may have fallen upon him, as one has expressed it, "in shreds and tatters," his utterances are nevertheless those of a profoundly stirred heart speaking out of an agitated situation.

His aim redeems his style.   Though he uses a limited
vocabulary, and frequently repeats the same
formulas, yet he was profoundly in earnest and must
be acknowledged as not wanting in force when he
exhorts, or in pathos when he reproves.   "A
prophet's historical magnitude is measured, not by
the literary splendor of his style, but by the work that
he accomplishes" (Elmslie).

SPECIAL LITERATURE ON HAGGAI

W. E. Barnes, "Haggai and Zechariah," "*Cambridge Bible* (1917); M. Dods, "Haggai, Zechariah
and Malachi," *Handbooks for Bible Classes;* T. V.
Moore, *Haggai, Zechariah and Malachi* (1856);
W. Drake, "Haggai and Zechariah," *Speaker's Commentary* (1876); Tony André, *Le Prophète Aggèe*
(1895); J. P. Lange, *Die Propheten Haggai, Sacharja, and Maleachi* (1876); E. Sellin, *Studien zur
Entstehungsgeschichte der jüdischen Gemeinde,* ii
(1901); K. Budde, "Zum Text der drei letzten
kleinen Propheten," *ZATW.* (1906); W. Böhme,
Zatw. (1887); J. W. Rothstein, *Juden und Samari-
taner* (1908).

CHAPTER XI

ZECHARIAH THE SEER

I. *Genealogy and Mission.*—In the introduction to his book, Zechariah is spoken of as "the son of Berechiah, the son of Iddo" (1:1, 7), but in Ezra 5:1; 6:14, as simply "the son of Iddo"; yet, doubtless, the same prophet is referred to in both passages. In the latter he is referred to as a contemporary of Haggai, which accords perfectly with the dates assigned to the prophecies of both these seers in their respective books (Hag. 1:1; 2:10; Zech. 1:1, 7) for their mission was in general the same, namely, that of inducing the people to rebuild the Temple. Zechariah was probably Haggai's junior (cf. Zech. 2:4; Hag. 2:3), and a man of unusual, almost unparalleled, vision. Being a priest as well as a prophet (Neh. 12:16), and the head of a "father's house," his influence was very great. His name, indeed, hints of special endowment; his name in Hebrew meaning, "he whom Jehovah remembers."

II. *General Character of His Book.*—Few books of the Old Testament are as difficult of interpretation as that of Zechariah. Jewish expositors like Abarbanel and Jarchi, and Christian interpreters such as Jerome, have been forced to concede that they failed "to find their hands" in the exposition of the prophet's visions (using a Hebrew idiom

147

found in Ps. 76:5), and that they passed from one labyrinth to another, and from one cloud into another until they were lost. And, indeed, the scope of the prophet's vision and the spiritual profundity of his thought challenge the most earnest reflection. In fact, it is no exaggeration to affirm that of all the prophetic compositions of the Old Testament, Zechariah's visions and oracles are the most messianic, and, accordingly, the most difficult, because mingled and intermingled with so much that is apocalyptic and eschatological.

III. *His Times.*—The earliest date in his book is "the second year of Darius," i.e., the second year of Darius Hystaspis, which is known to have been 520 B.C., and the latest is "the fourth year" of the same king's reign (Zech. 1:1, 7; 7:1), but it is of course quite possible that the prophet continued preaching and exhorting until at least the Temple was completed in the year 516 B.C. (Ezra 6:15). The circumstances and conditions under which Zechariah labored were in general those of Haggai's times, for Haggai began to preach just two months prior to Zechariah (cf. Hag. 1:1; Zech. 1:1). It was the year 520 B.C. About that time there were repeated upheavals and commotions throughout the length and breadth of the Persian Empire. The statement, in Zech. 1:11, that "all the earth sitteth still, and is at rest," was true only in the sense that all opposition to the Jews in rebuilding their Temple was at an end. With the accession of Darius in 521 B.C., as is well known, many of the tribes which had been forced to submit to Persian domination under Cyrus and Cambyses became rebellious. Insurrections broke out all over the empire, especially in the northeast, and Darius was compelled to fight some nineteen battles before the recalcitrant tribes were subdued.

But Jeremiah's predictions regarding the domination of Babylon, for "seventy years," had been fulfilled (Jer. 25:11; 29:10), and 42,360 Jews had returned in 536 B.C. to Jerusalem under the leadership of Zerubbabel and Joshua. Work on the Temple had been started, but the opposition of their neighbors had caused them to postpone the completion of the holy structure, and they had grown disheartened and depressed because they had not been able to restore Zion. The foundations of the Temple had been long laid, but as yet there was no superstructure (Ezra 3:8-10; Zech. 1:16). The altar of burnt-offering had been set up upon its former site, but there were as yet no priests worthy to officiate in the ritual of sacrifice (Ezra 3:2, 3; Zech. 3:3).

The people had grown apathetic and required to be roused to their obligation to complete the sanctuary. Haggai had already given them an impulse forward (Hag. 1:1, 15), but it was left to Zechariah to bring the task of Temple-building to completion. This he successfully accomplished, for the house was finished "in the sixth year of the reign of Darius," or 516 B.C. (Ezra 6:14, 15).

IV. *Analysis and Contents.*—The prophecies of Zechariah naturally fall into two parts; chaps. 1-8 and 9-14, both of which begin with the present and look apocalyptically forward into the future.

1. Chapters 1-8 consist of three distinct messages which were delivered on three separate occasions:

(a) Chapter 1:1-6, an introduction, delivered in

the eighth month of the second year of Darius (520 B.C.). It strikes the keynote of the entire book, and is one of the strongest and most intensely spiritual calls to repentance to be found anywhere in the Old Testament.

(b) Chapters 1:7-6:15, a series of eight symbolic night-visions, followed by a coronation scene; all delivered on the twenty-fourth day of the eleventh month of the second year of Darius, which was exactly two months after the corner stone of the Temple had been laid (Hag. 2:18; Zech. 1:7). These eight visions were intended to encourage the post-exilic colony in Jerusalem to continue and complete the construction of God's house, and they teach severally the following lessons:

(1) *The heavenly couriers* (1:7-17); teaching God's special care for and interest in his people, and affirming explicitly, "my house shall be built" (vs. 16).

(2) *The four horns and the four smiths* (1:18-21); teaching that Israel's foes have finally through war destroyed themselves, and that there is no longer any opposition to the building of God's house.

(3) *The man with a measuring line in his hand* (chap. 2); teaching that God will repeople, protect, and dwell in Jerusalem, and that the city will expand until it becomes a metropolis, without walls; indeed, that Jehovah himself will be the glory in the midst of, and a wall of fire round about, it.

(4) *Joshua the high priest, clad in filthy garments, bearing the sins of himself and of his people* (chap. 3); teaching that the priesthood shall

be cleansed, continued, and made typical of the Messiah-Branch to come, in whose day the iniquity of the land will be wholly taken away.

(5) *The golden candelabrum and the two olive trees* (chap. 4); teaching that the visible must give place to the spiritual, and that through "the two sons of oil," namely Zerubbabel the layman, and Joshua the ecclesiastic (vs. 14), the light of God's Temple will burn with ever flaming brightness; for it is "not by might nor by power," but by Jehovah's spirit that his house shall realize its end (vs. 6).

(6) *The flying roll* (5:1-4); teaching that God has in his law pronounced a curse upon wickedness, and intends to "cut off" sinners.

(7) *The ephah* (chap. 5:5-11); describing wickedness as personified and borne away, far back to the land of Shinar, and teaching that when the Temple is rebuilt, sin shall actually be removed from the land.

(8) *The four chariots* (6:1-8); issuing from the presence of the Lord of all the earth, and teaching that God's protecting providence will be over his people and their sanctuary, even though the city's walls may need a Nehemiah to repair them.

These visions are followed by a coronation scene (6:9-15), in which Joshua, the high priest, is crowned and made typical of the Messiah-Branch-Priest-King—the most composite and complete portrait of the Coming One to be found in the Old Testament.

(c) Chapters 7-8, Zechariah's answer to the Bethel deputation concerning fasting, delivered on the fourth day of the ninth month of the fourth year of Darius, 518 B.C. Since the downfall of

Jerusalem in 586 B.C., the Jews had been accustomed to fast on the anniversaries of four great outstanding events in their history: (1) When Nebuchadnezzar took Jerusalem in the fourth month (Jer. 52:6); (2) when the Temple was burnt in the fifth month (Jer. 52:12); (3) when Gedeliah, the governor, was murdered in the seventh month (Jer. 41:1, 2); and (4) when the siege of Jerusalem was begun in the tenth month (II Kings 25:1).

The prophet in his reply to the Bethel deputation emphasizes that Israel's fasts shall, instead of fasts, become festivals, and that many nations shall join with them in seeking the Lord of hosts in Jerusalem (Zech. 8:18-23).

2. Chapters 9-14 constitute the second part of the book, and are made up of two "burdens," or oracles, without dates:

(a) Chapters 9-11, *an oracle of promise to the new Theocracy.* In general, this section contains promises of a land in which to dwell, a return from exile, victory over a hostile world-power, also temporal blessings and national strength, and closes with a parable of judgment brought on by Israel's rejection of Jehovah and their shepherd. More specifically, in chap. 9, Judah and Ephraim restored, united, and made victorious over their enemies, are promised a land and a king; in chap. 10, Israel is to be saved and strengthened; in chap. 11, Israel is to be punished for rejecting the shepherding care of Jehovah.

(b) Chapters 12-14 contain *an oracle describing the victories of the new Theocracy and the coming day of the Lord.* This section is emphatically eschatological, presenting three distinct apocalyptic pictures: thus, in chap. 12, how Jerusalem shall be besieged by her enemies, but saved by Jehovah's intervention; in chap. 13, how a remnant of Israel, purified and refined, shall be saved; and in chap. 14, how the nations, after besieging and taking the city, shall stream up to Jerusalem and together keep the joyous Feast of Tabernacles; and how everything, in that day, even "the bells of the horses" and "every pot in Jerusalem and in Judah" shall become holy, i.e., dedicated to Jehovah; the whole section being a grand apocalyptic vision of judgment and redemption.

V.   *Abiding Lessons Taught by Zechariah*

1. How the drooping faith of a community may be revived through the preaching of a sincere and earnest prophet, who, though no genius, is possessed of "a soaring faith." Zechariah saw the possibility of a sudden and decisive intervention on the part of Jehovah in behalf of Israel.

2. How, as early as in Zechariah's time, "the former prophets" were already appealed to as normative and authentic (1:4; 7:12; cf. II Tim. 3:16, 17). Their writings were apparently already becoming canonical.

3. How the Jews, from the time of their first return, began to realize that the true religion would some day become world-wide (2:11; 6:15; 8:23; 14:16).

4. How the rebuilding of God's house was an indispensable condition of a better era (1:16). The prophet speaks frequently of God's "house";

five times in the first part (1:16; 3:7; 4:9; 7:3; 8:9), and four times in the second (9:8; 11:13; 14:20, 21). There can be no permanent social blessedness without the church!

5. How Israel's contest was really with Satan, their spiritual enemy, rather than with neighboring nations (3:1). Satan is always the chief assailant of the church.

6. How it behooves believers ever to hope beyond hope; though the flickering light of the church may burn dim betimes, yet it is "not by might, nor by power, but by my spirit, saith the Lord of hosts" (4:6).

7. How fasting and even feasting are nothing in themselves; for neither of these caused or averted Israel's Exile; what God requires of his people is the doing of justice and mercy, truth and righteousness (8:16, 17).

8. How God is willing to shepherd his unworthy sheep, taking two rods, instead of the single shepherd's crook, in order that he might devote himself in a manner not common to the office of shepherd; so solicitous is he for his people's welfare (11:7).

9. How the rebellious flock will mourn, so soon as they acknowledge that they are at war with God; for, as Calvin suggests, except a sinner sets himself in a manner before God's tribunal, he is never touched by a true feeling of repentance (12:10; cf. John 19:37).

10. How, finally, the contest between good and evil will end in one glorious day for Israel, when the Messiah comes and establishes his Kingdom, and Jehovah will be king over all the earth; and there shall be no more curse (14:9, 11); "It shall

be one day which is known unto Jehovah; not day and not night; but it shall come to pass, that at evening time there shall be light" (14:7). Herein is found true optimism!

SPECIAL LITERATURE ON ZECHARIAH

1. *In Defense of the Unity of the Book:* C. H. H. Wright, *Zechariah and His Prophecies* (1879); G. L. Robinson, *The Prophecies of Zechariah, with Special Reference to the Origin and Date of Chapters 9-14,* Leipzig dissertation, reprinted from the *American Journal of Semitic Languages and Literatures,* XII (1896); W. H. Lowe, *The Hebrew Students' Commentary on Zechariah* (1882); C. J. Bredenkamp, *Der Prophet Zach.* (1879); Marcus Dods, "Haggai, Zechariah and Malachi," *Handbooks for Bible Classes* (1879); E. P. Pusey, *The Minor Prophets* (1877); W. Drake, "Commentary on Zechariah," *Speaker's Commentary* (1876); T. W. Chambers, "Commentary on Zechariah," *Lange's Bible Work* (1874); A. van Hoonacher, "Les chapitres ix-xiv du livre Zecharie," *Revue Biblique* (1902); A. von Hoonacher, *Les douze petits prophètes* (1908); William Moeller, "Zechariah," *Illustrated Bible Dictionary* (1908).

2. *In Favor of a Pre-exilic Origin for Chapters 9-14:* Hitzig-Steiner, *Die zwölf kl. Propheten* (1881); S. Davidson, *Introduction to the Old Testament,* (1862-63); W. Pressel, *Kommentar zu Hag., Sach. u. Mal.* (1870); E. Bruston, *Histoire critique de la littérature prophétique des Hebreux* (1881); C. von Orelli, "Die zwölf kleinen Propheten," *Kurzgefasster Kommentar* (3rd ed.,

1908; Eng. transl., 1893); E. Montet, *Étude critique sur la date assignable aux six dernier chapitres de Zecharie* (1882); H. L. Strack, *Einleitung in das A. T.* (1895); F. W. Farrar, "The Minor Prophets," *Men of the Bible Series*.

3. *Those Who Advocate a Post-Zecharian Origin for Chapters 9-14:* B. Stade, "Deuterozacharja," *Zeit. für Altest. Wissenschaft* (1881-82); T. K. Cheyne, "The Date of Zechariah, 9-14," *Jewish Quarterly Review* (1889); *ibid., Critica Biblica,* II (1903); C. H. Cornill, *Einleitung in die kanonischen Bücher des A. T.* (6th ed., 1908; Eng. transl. 1907); S. R. Driver, *Introduction to the Literature of the Old Testament* (1910); J. Wellhausen, *Die kl. Propheten* (1893); N. I. Rubinkam, *The Second Part of the Book of Zechariah* (1892); K. Marti, *Der Prophet Sacharja, der Zeitgenosse Zerubbabels* (1892); *ibid.,* "Zwei Studien zu Sacharja," *Stud. u. Krit.* (1892); *ibid., Dodekapropheten* (1904); *ibid.,* "Die Zweifel an der prophetischen Sendung Sacharja's," in the Wellhausen *Festschrift* (1914); A. F. Kirkpatrick, *The Doctrine of the Prophets* (1892); R. Eckhardt, "Der Sprachgebrauch von Zach., 9-14," *ZATW.* (1893); A. K. Kuiper, *Zacharia ix-xiv, eine exegelische-critische Studie* (1894); J. W. Rothstein, *Die Nachtgesichte des Sacharja* (1910); G. A. Smith, "The Book of the Twelve Prophets," *Expositors' Bible,* II (2d ed., 1898); H. G. Mitchell, *Int. Critical Commentary* (1912); E. Sellin, *Introduction to the Old Testament* (Eng. transl. 1923); V. D. Flier, "Sach. 1-8," *Theolog. Stud. u. Kritiken* (1906); Grützmacher, *Untersuchung über die Ursprung von Sach. 9-14* (1892).

CHAPTER XII

MALACHI THE LECTURER

I. *The Name of the Author.*—Nothing is known
of the person of Malachi apart from the book which
bears his name.   As he was the last of the Old
Testament prophets, *a priori,* we should expect him
to have been well known to the collectors of the
canon.   The fact, however, that his name does not
occur elsewhere in the Old Testament leads some to
doubt whether "Malachi" was ever intended as the
personal name of the prophet.   But, since Aquilla,
Symmachus, and Theodotian in the second century
A.D., "Malachi" has been generally regarded as a
proper name.   No one of the other Old Testament
prophets is anonymous.

The name signifies "my messenger," and corre-
sponds exactly in form to the "my messenger" in
Mal. 3:1; cf. 2:7.   Linguistically, *malâkhi* may
reasonably be regarded as an abbreviation of *malâ-
khiyâh,* meaning "messenger of Jehovah."   The
prophet Haggai is expressly designated a "messenger of Jehovah" (Hag. 1:13).   But the name
"Malachi" may, indeed, have been a mere appellation, or a *nom de guerre,* borne by the prophet, not
from his birth of course, but only from his call to
the prophetic office; for Malachi, of all the prophets, must have been a spiritual hero to attack the

priesthood as he did! The meaning of his name is therefore significant.

The title of his book, also, is suggestive. The opening phrase, "The burden of the word of Jehovah" (1:1) is found likewise in Zech. 9:1; 12:1, and nowhere else, in exactly this form, in the entire Old Testament; hence presumably emphatic, though it may be the work of an editor. The Septuagint adds "by the hand of *his messenger*"; and the Targum of Jonathan, "by the hand of *my angel,* whose name is called Ezra the scribe." Jerome likewise designates the book as Ezra's. Certain other traditions ascribe it to Zerubbabel and Nehemiah; and others still, to Malachi, whom they designate as a Levite and a member of the "Great Synagogue."

Perhaps, therefore, the best explanation of the name "Malachi" is to take it as adjectival and equivalent to the Latin *Angelicus,* signifying "one charged with a message or mission," hence a missionary (cf. the name "Haggai", meaning Festus). The name thus resolves itself into an official title appropriate to one whose message closes and seals, so to speak, the prophetic canon of the Old Testament. Fortunately the identity of the author is not essential for the authentication of his message. In any case the writer was a strong and vigorous personality.

II. *The Period of the Prophet.*—The book is silent as to the date of its composition. Opinions vary (Winckler assigning it to the period just before the Maccabean revolt), but it is almost universally allowed that the author was a contemporary of Ezra and Nehemiah, and wrote either about 458 or 432

B.C. Sellin, however, prefers to date him earlier, at "about 470 B.C." The social conditions portrayed are unquestionably those of the Persian period. The Temple, which had been rebuilt and dedicated in 516 B.C., was standing, and the routine of sacrifice had been long in operation. The Edomites were apparently still in exile, having been expelled from their home in the mountains by the Nabathæans shortly after the downfall of Jerusalem in 586 B.C. Serious abuses had crept into Jewish life; the priests had become lax and degenerate, defective sacrifices were allowed to be offered upon the temple altar, the people were neglecting their tithes, divorce was common, Jehovah's covenant was forgotten, and the people had grown skeptical of his righteousness, questioning sincerely their adoption as the peculiar people of his choice. These, we know, were precisely the conditions which prevailed also in Nehemiah's day (cf. Neh. 3:5; 5:1-13).

It is the opinion of many, however, that Malachi could not have prophesied during Nehemiah's *active* governorship; for in Mal. 1:8 it is implied that gifts might be offered to the "governor," whereas Nehemiah tells us that he himself declined to exact all official dues (Neh. 5:15, 18). But, per contra, as Elmslie correctly observes, "a gift to ingratiate the giver is quite another thing, and, moreover, the reference is not personal or local, but general and purely illustrative." The abuses which the prophet attacks correspond unquestionably to those which Nehemiah attempted to correct on his second visit to Jerusalem in 432 B.C. (Neh. 13:7 ff.). That Malachi should exhort the people to remember the law of Moses, which was publicly read by Ezra in

the year 444 B.C., is in perfect agreement with this
conclusion, despite the fact that Stade, Cornill,
Kautzsch, W. R. Smith, and others argue, on the
basis of the alleged late publication of this law, for
an earlier date prior to the time of Ezra (458 B.C.).
With better judgment Nägelsbach, Köhler, Orelli,
Volck, and a host of others, assign the origin of the
book to the period between the two visits of Nehemiah to Jerusalem in 445 and 432 B.C. But, whatever our conclusion may be as to its exact setting,
the book of Malachi is a significant landmark in
the religious history of Israel during the reign of
Artaxerxes, king of Persia, who reigned from 465
till 425 B.C.

III. *The Author's Style.*—The unity of Malachi's
little book (only 55 verses) is not disputed. He
was content to write in prose, though he is seldom
prosaic. The expression "saith Jehovah of hosts"
occurs some twenty times. His Hebrew is pure and
comparatively free of Aramaisms.

Whether Malachi ever delivered as sermons the
contents of his book is difficult to say. In any case
the substantial elements which compose it are closely
knit together, being the work obviously of a legal
pleader and of a moral reasoner who had a definite
and detailed plan of argument. His style is doubtless inferior to that of some of the pre-exilic prophets, yet he possesses a vigor and force which they
seldom surpass. Occasionaly he reveals touches of
prophetic imagination worthy of his predecessors;
even poetic rhythm and parallelism (cf. 1:11; 3:1,
6, 10; 4:1). His figures are always chaste and
beautiful (cf. 1:6; 3:2, 3; 4:1-3).

Malachi's literary method was that of the scribes,

putting and answering questions. "The form of his book shows us that his period was no longer patient of prophetic preachers; he has to have recourse to argument" (Sellin). He was the Hebrew Socrates. This style was novel among the Jews. It is known as the didactic-dialectic method. First he makes a charge or an accusation; then he fancies some one raises an objection, which he next proceeds to refute in detail, substantiating the truth of his original proposition. Seven distinct examples of this peculiar method of (a) affirmation, (b) interrogation, and (c) refutation are to be found in his little book (the expression "Yet ye say," 1:2, 6, 7; 2:14, 17; 3:7, 8, 13, occurring eight times), for example:

1. I have loved you, saith Jehovah.
    Yet ye say, Wherein hast thou loved us?
    In that Jacob was *disciplined* only—being brought from exile;
    Whereas Esau was *punished*—being left in captivity (1:2, 3).

2. You priests despise my name, offering polluted bread.
    Yet ye say, wherein have we polluted thee?
    In that ye say, The table of Jehovah is contemptible (1:6, 7).

3. Ye have profaned the covenant of your fathers.
    Yet ye say, Wherein have we done so?
    In that ye deal treacherously with the wife of thy covenant (2:10-16).

4. Ye have wearied Jehovah with your words.
   Yet ye say, Wherein have we wearied him?
   In that ye say, Evil is good, and good, evil
      (2:17).

5. Ye have turned aside from mine ordinances.
   But ye say, Wherein shall we return (3:7)?
   (Malachi wastes no time in answering, as their
      question is insincere).

6. Ye have robbed God.
   But ye say, Wherein have we robbed thee?
   In tithes and offerings (3:8).

7. Your words have been stout against me, saith
      Jehovah.
   Yet ye say, What have we spoken against thee?
   Ye have said, It is vain to serve God (3:13, 14).

This debating, lecture-like style is peculiarly characteristic of Malachi. He shows clearly the influence of the schools, and is on the way to the Talmud. Besides, his employment of "also" (1:13) and "again" (2:13), which is equivalent to our "firstly" and "secondly," is additional evidence to the same effect. Yet, notwithstanding the mechanical uniformity under which he labors and the abrupt transitions which he makes from one theme to another, his prophecies are full of vigor and forcefulness, and he drives home old truth with singular originality and earnestness. His book may be fairly classed as the most argumentative of all Old Testament prophecies.

IV. *Contents of Malachi.*—The book opens with
a clear, sharp statement of the prophet's chief thesis,
that Jehovah still loves Israel (1:2-5); and it closes
with an earnest word of exhortation to remember
the law of Moses (4:4-6). The body of the book
is composed of two extended polemics against (1)
the unfaithful priests, who have become lax and
indifferent in their ministrations of the sanctuary
(1:6-2:9); and (2) the unfaithful people, who have
begun to doubt both Jehovah's love and his providence (2:10-4:3). "There are two special objects
of his censure, the unworthy way in which the cultus
was practiced, for which the priests are above all
to blame, and the putting away on frivolous pre-
texts of Jewish wives, with its correlative of mixed
marriages with the heathen. On account of these he
sees the day of Jehovah's judgment drawing near"
(Sellin). Apart from the title or superscription
(1:1), the book falls naturally into the following
seven divisions:

1. Chapter 1:2-5, in which the prophet shows that
Jehovah still loves Israel, because Israel's lot stands
in such marked contrast to Edom's. Israel, though
exiled, has been brought back from captivity, having
been only temporarily disciplined; Edom, on the
contrary, has been permanently driven out of its
mountain fastnesses, and will never return—being
irretrievably and inexorably banished!

2. Chapters 1:6-2:9, a denunciation of the
priests, the Levites, who have become neglectful of
their sacerdotal office, indifferent to the Law, and un-
mindful of their covenant relationship to Jehovah.
Better to shut the doors of the temple, exclaims
the prophet, than to offer such sacrifices in such a

heartless manner! Malachi is an intensely earnest
preacher of repentance.

3. Chapter 2:10-16, a trenchant rebuke to the
people for their idolatry and divorce. This section
can hardly be interpreted as merely metaphorical of
Israel's having abandoned the religion of his youth.
On the contrary, the people are obviously rebuked
for putting away, literally, their own Jewish wives
in order to contract marriage with foreigners. Such
marriages, the prophet declares, are not only a form
of idolatry, but a violation of Jehovah's desire to
preserve a "godly seed" (vss. 11, 14, 15).

4. Chapters 2:17-3:6, an announcement of coming judgment. Men had come to doubt seriously
whether there was longer a God of justice (vs.
17b). Malachi responds in messianic language of
great significance, saying that the Lord whom the
people seek will suddenly come to judgment, both
to purify the sons of Levi and to purge the land
of sinners in general. Yet, because of Jehovah's
unchangeableness, the sons of Jacob will not be
utterly consumed (3:6).

5. Chapter 3:7-12, in which the prophet pauses
to give another concrete example of the people's
sins: they have failed to pay their tithes and other
dues. Accordingly drought, locusts, and famine
have ensued. But let them pay their dues in full,
and their land will become "a delightsome land."

6. Chapters 3:13-4:3, a second section addressed
to the doubters of the prophet's age. In 2:17 they
had said, "Where is the God of justice?" They
now murmur, "It is vain to serve God; and what
profit is it, that we have kept his charge?" The
wicked prosper as well as the good (3:14,15).

But, the prophet replies, Jehovah knows them that are his, and a book of remembrance is being kept of all those who fear Jehovah and encourage one another in faith (3:16);—here we have the germ possibly of the later synagogue; for, when the day of judgment comes and the good and evil are distinguished, those who have worked iniquity will be exterminated, while upon those who do righteously and fear Jehovah's name, "the sun of righteousness" (heavenly radium!) will arise with healing in its wings.

7. Chapter 4 : 4-6, a concluding exhortation to obey the Mosaic Law; with a promise that Elijah the prophet will first come to avert, if possible, the threatened judgment by reconciling the hearts of the people to one another, i.e., by reconciling the ideals of the old generation to those of the new (vs. 6). This statement that Elijah will come to urge repentance (as the Law can only condemn) is a tacit confession by Malachi that prophecy is about to cease.

V. *Malachi's Message Evaluated*.—Being an intense patriot, Malachi's language was accordingly clean cut and correspondingly exacting. His primary aim to his own age was to encourage an already disheartened people who were presumably disappointed that Haggai's and Zechariah's optimistic predictions concerning the messianic kingdom had not been fulfilled. A serious reaction had set in and men were beginning to doubt God's providence. A new reformation was necessary.

On the other hand, his spiritual aim was to prepare the way for the coming of the Messiah. To do this he emphasized the following major points:

1. *The true value of ritual* (1:6 ff.).—Malachi
like Haggai, lays great emphasis upon ritual—
honest ritual; perfunctory or half-hearted ritual
he abhors. He calls the people to moral and
religious earnestness and insists upon purity and
sincerity in public worship. The earlier prophets
had denounced slavish adherence to ritual when it
usurped the place of the true spiritual and ethical worship of Jehovah. But circumstances had
changed in Malachi's times, and he found it necessary to insist upon the proper observance of the
ceremonial law. Likewise to him the ceremonial
law was of no value in itself, except as it expressed
worship, and reverence, and obedience. Empty
ritual was worse than no worship at all; better that
the doors of the Temple were shut (1:10); and
he adds:

"For from the rising of the sun unto the going
down of the same my name (shall be) great among
the Gentiles; and in every place incense (shall be)
offered unto my name, and a pure offering; for my
name (shall be) great among the Gentiles saith
Jehovah of hosts" (1:11).

This passage is frequently interpreted as a recognition on Malachi's part of the religious earnestness
of the Gentiles, and as a tribute to the truer and
better side of *heathen* religion. Driver, for example, uses it as a text in preaching on "Compara-
tive Religion" (*Ideals of the Prophets,* 1915);
Ottley, also, as a form of pagan devotion which
Jehovah is willing to accept (*The Religion of Israel,*
1905). But the phrase "my name," used thrice in
the verse, renders this interpretation highly improbable. Malachi's point is rather this: The Jews

of the diaspora, beyond the limits of Palestine, scattered throughout the heathen world, wherever Jewish colonies are to be found (as at that time on the island of Elephantine in Upper Egypt), bring sacrifices to Jehovah, which, as expressions of honest worship, put to shame the half-hearted and worthless worship of the unwilling priests in Jerusalem. As J. M. P. Smith observes: "It is quite evident that the writer of this prophecy may have shared the views of the colonists as to the legitimacy of sacrificial worship upon foreign soil and may have had such shrines as that at Elephantine in mind when he wrote." Malachi was no mere formalist.

2. *The crime of divorce* (2:10 ff.).—To Malachi wanton divorce was a sin against the love of Jehovah and a crime against the brotherhood of man. It meant the breaking of God's sacred covenant; it involved idolatry; it was treachery to the wife of one's youth, and thwarted, through destroying the sanctity of the home, God's purpose of securing to himself a "godly seed." The climax of the prophet's argument is found in 2:15: "And did he not make one, although he had the residue of the Spirit? And wherefore one? He sought a godly seed."

In any case Malachi was a Christian on the subject of divorce; for, "No higher word on marriage was ever spoken except by Christ himself" (G. A. Smith).

3. *The coming of the Messiah and his Kingdom* (3:1 ff.).—Malachi's messianic teaching is very simple: the Kingdom of God, he taught, will be preceded by the "day of Jehovah" which will be the occasion of purifying and refining. Jehovah him-

self will usher it in. "Behold I send my messenger, and he shall prepare the way before me: and the Lord, whom ye seek, will suddenly come to his temple: and (better, "even") the messenger of the covenant, whom ye desire, behold he cometh, saith Jehovah of hosts" (3:1).

This striking messianic utterance was occasioned by the people's doubts as to whether Jehovah were really still a God of justice (2:17). Malachi constructs for them a new theodicy; and yet it is not new, for Isaiah had already taught the doctrine of a faithful remnant. Joel's "day of Jehovah" has been delayed, but the delay is due entirely to Jehovah's love. Even yet he will send Elijah, the great advocate of religious decision, to heal the dissensions in the nation before the coming of that great and terrible day (4:6). The assurance here that the dawn of a Golden Age was at hand must have greatly encouraged the drooping spirits and wavering faith of the Jewish people. Malachi believed most firmly that in due time a Divine Deliverer would come; according¹ he vehemently urges the people to believe still in their own future. The apocalyptic character of chaps. 3:13-4:2 is fine!

4. *The eternal discipline of the Law* (4:4-6).— Malachi lays final emphasis upon the necessity of keeping the Mosaic Law. Earlier in his prophecies he had rebuked the priests, who were the custodians and expounders of the Law, for having caused many to stumble (2:7, 8); and he had also warned the people that obedience to the Law is the only sure path of blessing, pointing out to them with almost dramatic emphasis that the reason a curse remained on the nation's labors was because they had for-

gotten the Law (2:17-3:12). It is plainly evident
that the people were already beginning to feel the
effects of their more intimate acquaintance with the
great nations round about them. Ancient rites and
old beliefs were becoming more and more outgrown. Malachi met this tendency by exalting the
Law of Moses, which had been the real cause of
their national strength. Malachi was no creator,
but he knew how to conserve the spiritual inheritance of the past. "To understand the Law is easy;
to appraise it is a much harder task" (Welch).
With Malachi, no less than with Christ himself, not
one jot or tittle should everr pass away or become
obsolete.

SPECIAL LITERATURE ON MALACHI

Beside the *Commentaries on the Twelve Minor
Prophets* already recommended in the introduction
of this volume; and *Old Testament Introductions;*
and articles on "Malachi" in the various *Bible Dictionaries,* and *Encyclopædias;* see also, A. Köhler,
Die Weissagungen Maleachis (1865); A. Bachmann, *Alttestamentliche Untersuchungen* (1894);
H. Winckler, *Altorientalische Forschungen,* ii,
(1901).

APPENDIX
CRITICAL NOTES

APPENDIX

CRITICAL NOTES

I

DISPUTED PASSAGES IN HOSEA

A few radical critics, misled by W. R. Harper in the *International Critical Commentary,* eliminate, ruthlessly, all of Hosea's promises of the future, which they attribute to later post-exilic interpolators. Accordingly, Hosea is left a prophet of gloom and of doom, without any gospel at all, having "promised nothing," as Harper says, and having painted a future altogether dark. The following passages by such critics are denied to Hosea: 1 :1, 7; 1 :10-2 :1; 2 : 4, 6, 7, 10, 14-16, 18-23; 3 : 5; 4 :15, 16; 5 : 5; 6 : 10, 11; 7 :1, 4; 8 :10, 14 : 9 : 9; 10 : 3, 4, 10; 11 : 11; 12 :3-6, 12, 13; 14 :1-9; i.e., 48 out of 197 verses are rejected; or, approximately one-fourth of the entire book. The reasons given for denying the genuineness of all these noble passages, is because, forsooth, they interrupt the order of the prophet's thought, are in some cases repetitions and too eschatological, and are inconsistent with the rhythm and strophic structure of the prophet's own language. But it is perfectly obvious to thoughtful minds that such reasoning is too subjective and inconclusive. "There is no reason for re-writing Hosea at will, as is done in measure by Dr. Harper, and without measure by Prof. Cheyne," as Melville Scott pertinently remarks! Strange that later redactors felt it necessary to add to Hosea's messages others of their own so alien to the prophet's intention as actually to contradict it! More recent critics are coming to recognize the arbitrary character of such reasoning. As Sellin observes, "This whole criticism rests on completely false premises. The expectation of deliverance is no new idea with Hosea. What wonder, therefore, that the expectation of a final deliverance should run like a red cord through his book?" With Baumgartner, Sellin adduces positive arguments in favor of the genuineness of all the prophecies of salvation enunciated by Hosea. Driver does the same, adding words of great significance: "It may be questioned whether recent criticism has not shown a tendency to limit unduly the spiritual capabilities and imaginative power of the pre-exilic prophets; and whether, the prophets being *poets*, guided often, as is clear, by impulse and feeling rather than by strict logic, imperfect connection with the context (except in extreme cases, or when supported by linguistic or other independent indications) forms a sufficient ground for judging a passage to be a later insertion. It is also not improbable that the discourses of the prophets have often been transmitted to us in a condensed form, in which meditating links may have been omitted. A picture of restoration, at the end of a prophecy, does not neutralize previous threatenings."

The last chapter of Hosea completes the prophet's picture of the final triumph of Jehovah's love.

It is not a prediction, but rather the prophet's final appeal to Israel, the sun and substance of his whole message.   It is the work of a real genius, and belongs just where it is found.   Nowack recognizes this.   Jeremiah was also a prophet of restoration. He was to Judah what Hosea was to Israel.   In fact, Jeremiah shows the influence of Hosea; many passages in Jeremiah being little less than a transscript of Hosea: e.g., compare Jer. 14:10 and Hos. 8:3; Jer. 4:3 and Hos. 10:12; Jer. 6:20 and Hos. 9:4.   Jeremiah was the spiritual heir of Hosea; but not of his book emasculated!

II

THE UNITY OF JOEL

The unity of the book of Joel is seldom challenged.   Even Merx regarded the whole book as one piece.   Yet Vernes, Rothstein, and a few others deny that it was produced by any one man in a single age.   Vernes, in 1872, was the first to question its unity, separating the four chapters (as divided in Hebrew) into equal halves; but in 1880 he was less confident of his opinion.   Rothstein, in 1896, assigned 1:1-2:27 to the reign of Joash; and 2:28-3:21 to a post-exilic date.   Bewer removes certain interpolations, and remarks, "Chapters 1-2 treat of a locust plague and drought, and contained originally no reference to the day of Jehovah; chaps. 3-4 (as divided in Hebrew) treat of the day of Jehovah, and contain no reference to the locust plague and the drought." Baudissin, also, suggests extensive revision.

According to Haupt, "The present tendency is to regard the book as composite." Haupt holds chaps. 1-2 are earlier than the Pentateuchal Codes JE, but that chaps. 3-4 (in Hebrew) date from ca. 130 B.C. He finds in the book nine separate poems, which the editors have mixed and pieced together, thus:

1. "The Locust Poem," referring figuratively to Syrian invaders in comparatively ancient pre-exilic times, before JE (i.e., in the ninth century B.C.); consisting of two main sections: (a) 2:2, 10, 4, 5, 7, 8, 9 (in this order) and (b) 1:2, 5, 6, 7, 18; 2:3b; two stanzas, each having four couplets, with 3+3 beats in each line.

2. A Poem, descriptive of Antiochus Epiphanes' spoliation of the temple in 170 B.C. (2:15, 16, 17; two triplets, with 3+3 beats in each line).

3. Another Poem, describing the suspension of the daily sacrifices in the temple, December, 168 B.C. (1:8, 9, 13, 14, 15; three couplets, with 3+3 beats in each line).

4. Another, telling of the famine in 161 B.C. (1:10, 11, 17, 16, 10, 12, three triplets, with 2+2 beats in each line).

5. A Contrasting Poem, describing the good fortune of Simon's reign, in two parts: (a) 2:21, 22, 23, 24; and (b) chap. 2:19a, 25, 26, 27, 19b; two stanzas, each having two triplets, with 3+3 beats in each line.

6. A Poem, telling of the threatened and impending invasion of Cendebræus, in two sections: (a) 2:12, 13; 3:1, 3; and (b) 2:1, 6, 11b, 2a, 11a; two

stanzas with two triplets each, having 3+3 beats in each line.

7. An Arraignment of Judah's enemies (3: 2, 4, 5, 6, 7, 8; four couplets, with 3+3 beats in each line).

8. A Dramatic Call to Battle, in two parts: (a) 4:9, 10, 11; and (b) 4:12, 13, 14, 17; two stanzas, each having triplets, with 2+2 beats in each line.

9. The Future Prosperity of Judah Predicted (3:18, 19; two triplets, with 3+3 beats). The Jews, Haupt would have us note, defeated the Syrians the very next day (I Macc. 16:8)! Yet, there is no mention of "Syria" in the entire book!

After such a jumbling and shaking up of the book, one is not surprised to learn that Haupt finds "no ethical teaching in Joel's prophecies; the religious and social ideals being all nationalistic; the several poems having been delivered, not to teach morality, but to contribute to the victory of Jewish arms!"

In our judgment no better proof of the unity of the book could be desired than this dissection of Joel by Haupt. What he really demonstrates by this elaborate and arbitrary analysis is the fallibility of criticism!

III

CRITICISM OF AMOS

For various reasons the following passages have been deleted from the original prophecies of Amos: 1:1, 2, 9-12; 2:4, 5, 12; 4:13-5:2; 5:8, 9, 15; 6:2,

14; 8:11-13; and 9:5, 6, 8-15. W. R. Harper
rejects, besides most of these, still other passages.
W. Robertson Smith and Kuenen, in their day, de-
fended the genuineness of 2:4, 5; 4:13; 5:8, 9; and
9:5, 6. The tendency today is to reclaim for Amos
many more passages still in dispute: for example,
Sellin finds no difficulty in allowing that Amos wrote
9:11-15, if only this section be allowed to stand
immediately after 7:10-17, as it probably did originally. Driver also treats this same section as
genuine. And even Professor McFadyen allows
that "It is altogether probable that the criticism of
the future will substantially restore to Amos verses
whose authenticity has been widely questioned."

The principal grounds alleged for rejecting those
passages in dispute are that they represent later
stages of history than the time of Amos, interrupt
the context, are unnecessary, and even in some cases
incompatible with the context. But sober minds do
not find it necessary to dissect the prophet's writings
quite so surgically. It certainly is as unreasonable in
the case of Amos as in that of Hosea to suppose
that he was exclusively a prophet of ruin. Amos has
his apparently pessimistic notes, but a true prophet
can never be a pessimist and a pessimist only. One
can not easily understand how a prophet of the type
of Amos could close his mission in absolute despair.
Repeatedly in his prophecies he exhorted Israel to
"Seek Jehovah and live" (5:4, 6, 8, 14); and certainly passages like 7:3, 6 prove that he saw rifts in
the clouds of divine judgment now and then.

IV

RELATION OF OBADIAH, vss. 1-9 TO JEREMIAH 49:7-22

The verbal relationship between these is too close to be accidental. Either Jeremiah quoted from Obadiah, or Obadiah quoted from Jeremiah, or both worked over and utilized an older prophecy. Here are some of the most striking parallels between them:

Obad., Vss. 1-9	Jer. 49:7-22
1. We have heard tidings from Jehovah, and an ambassador is sent among the nations, saying, Arise ye, and let us rise up against her in battle.	14. I have heard tidings from Jehovah, and an ambassador is sent among the nations, saying, Gather yourselves together, and come against her, and rise up to the battle.
2. Behold, I have made thee small among the nations; thou art greatly despised.	15. Behold I have made thee small among the nations, and despised among men.
3a. The pride of thy heart hath deceived thee, O thou that dwellest in the clefts of the rock whose habitation is high.	16a. The pride of thy heart hath deceived thee, O thou that dwellest in the clefts of the rock, that holdest the height of the hill.
4. Though thou mount on high as the eagle, and though thy nest be set among the stars, I will bring thee down from thence, saith Jehovah.	16b. Though thou shouldest make thy nest as high as the eagle, I will bring thee down from thence, saith Jehovah.

Obad., Vss. 1-9	Jer. 49: 7-22
5. If thieves come to thee, if robbers by night (how art thou cut off!) would they not steal only till they had enough? If grape gatherers came to thee, would they not leave some gleaning grapes?	9. If grape-gatherers came to thee, would they not leave some gleaning grapes? if thieves by night, would they not destroy till they had enough?
6. How are the things of Esau searched? how are his hidden treasures sought out?	10a. But I have made Esau bare, I have uncovered his secret places, and he shall not be able to hide himself.
8. Shall I not in that day, saith Jehovah, destroy the wise men out of Edom, and understanding out of the mount of Esau?	7. Thus saith Jehovah of hosts: Is wisdom no more in Teman? is counsel perished from the prudent? is their wisdom vanished?
9. And thy mighty men, O Teman, shall be dismayed.	22b. And the heart of the mighty men of Edom at that day shall be as the heart of a woman in her pangs.

If Jeremiah quoted from Obadiah, and if Jer. 49:7-22 was written by Jeremiah, then vss. 1-9 of our prophet must be pre-exilic. Most scholars, even modern text critics, believe they are. Says Sellin, "It is certain that Jer. 49:9 is quoted from Obd. 5 and not *vice versa*." But Hitzig and Vatke maintained that Jeremiah formed the model for Obadiah. More recently, Bewer, also, contends that "Obadiah quoted in vss. 1-9 an older oracle, the original of which is better preserved in Jer. chap. 49." But, from a literary and logical point of view, it must be admitted, if the prophecy is a unity, that the scales turn in favor of Obadiah's being the earlier and better text. His is the more natural and

forcible and the more graphic and compact; whereas
in Jeremiah there are vague *disjecti membra poetæ*
imbedded in what properly belongs to Obadiah; the
ideas are reversed in sequence, broken off from one
another, mingled with other matter, and so deprived
of their cumulative and orderly significance that but
one conclusion seems possible, namely, that Jeremiah
depended on Obadiah.   And this conclusion is overwhelmingly reinforced by the discovery that, in the
verses which Obadiah and Jeremiah have in common, there is not one idiom which occurs elsewhere
in Jeremiah.   "Now," says Pusey, "it would be
wholly improbable that a prophet selecting verses
out of the prophecies of Jeremiah should have
selected precisely these which contain none of Jeremiah's characteristic expressions."   Besides, it was
Jeremiah's custom to utilize older prophecies: cf.
his use of Isa. chaps. 15-16 in chap. 48.   Perhaps
Jeremiah, by resetting the words of Obadiah in his
own prophecy, wished, as Pusey also suggests, to
point out that the former prophecy was still in
force.

V

AUTHORSHIP, INTEGRITY, AND DATE OF JONAH

1. *Authorship:* The book is anonymous.   If not
written by Jonah, however, it is difficult to see why
the unknown author fixed on Jonah, rather than
upon Elijah, or some other prophet of Israel,   Jewish and Christian traditions are agreed in ascribing

it to Jonah himself. The abrupt beginning and the still more abrupt ending of the book seem to point in this direction. But it is quite possible, indeed probable, that someone who was conversant with Jonah's prophetic career composed the book a generation or more after Jonah's own time; moreover, it is written in the *third* person.

2. *Integrity:* According to Bewer, "not a single attempt to disintegrate Jonah is convincing. . . . The book is a unit except 2 :2-9, and several glosses." On the contrary, Nachtigal (1799), Kleinert, (1868), Köhler (1879), Böhme (1887), Winckler (1899), Schmidt (1905), and Erbt (1907), have all claimed to discover different sources in its composition, but without convincing success. Most critics, however, since Müller (1794), question the integrity of chap. 2. This chapter contains a hymn of thanksgiving presumably uttered in advance of the prophet's deliverance from the sea. It is a cento, or anthology, of different psalms, namely, Pss. 3, 18, 30, 31, 42, 50, 116, 120, and 142, so knit together as to form a beautiful mosaic. Saturated with psalm language, as Jonah may have been, this whole series of psalm quotations, as here recorded, could well have passed through the drowning man's mind in an instant of time, and been remembered too, as anyone knows, who has actually faced possible death by drowning, and then been delivered. Luther long ago had the good sense to see that "Jonah did not speak with these exact words in the belly of the fish; but they show how he took courage and what sort of thoughts his heart had when he stood in conflict with death." The poem is anything but "an anti-climax," or "a clumsy intrusion,"

as one expositor calls it. On the other hand, no one could have written it so naturally as he who had himself been delivered from a similar sea peril.

3. *Date:* If written by Jonah, then the book was composed ca. 780 B.C., as Jonah lived in the early part of Jeroboam's reign. But if the statement in 3:3, "Now Nineveh was a great city," implies (but it does not necessarily) that when the author wrote it was no longer in existence, then the *terminus a quo* is naturally the fall of Nineveh which took place in 606, or 611 B.C., according to the latest discoveries. On the other hand, the *terminus ad quem* will be the time of Jesus ben Sirach, who writing about 200 B.C., mentions Jonah by implication when he speaks of "the twelve prophets," Eccles. 49:10. The archæologist, Knight, in his very remarkable volume on archæology, entitled *Nile and Jordan,* 1921, page 344, calls attention to a seal belonging to the reign of Amasis II, 570-526 B.C., of Egyptian history, which shows a minute drawing, executed with remarkable clearness, of a man emerging from the mouth of a sea-monster, which Petrie identifies with Jonah; hence, the date of Jonah, Knight concludes, must be anterior to the time of Nebuchadnezzar. Such a date would confirm its order among the Twelve, which in the Hebrew is fifth, and in the Septuagint, sixth; in both, prior to Nahum and Habakkuk. Perhaps a date, therefore, about the middle of the seventh century B.C. would not be far from correct.

Modern critics, however, are almost unanimous in favor of a late post-exilic date. Here are the chief reasons for this opinion: (a) The book seems to represent a reaction to the exclusive teaching of

Ezra and Nehemiah, and was written, therefore, with the express aim of defending the duty of missions to the heathen; but this is pure fancy. (b) The piling up of marvelous features and wonders in quite the style of Chronicles and Daniel; but this proves nothing. (c) There is little doubt but the story is much older than the book; which may or may not be so. (d) The doctrine of universal grace as inculcated by the Book of Jonah is more in keeping with a late date; but the same doctrine is taught by Isa. 2:2-4; Mic. 4:1-5; and Amos 9:12; cf. Acts 10:43. (e) The use of the expression "the king of Nineveh," 3:6, instead of "the king of Assyria" points to a time after the fall of the city, rather than before; but this expression has many parallels of different dates, cf. "the king of Damascus," II Chron. 24:23; the "king of Heshbon," Deut. 2:26; and the "king of Samaria," I Kings 21:1. (f) The book contains certain Aramaisms, e.g., the expressions "God of heaven," 1:9; "proclamation," 3:7; "ship," 1:5; "think," 1:6; "prepared," 1:17; "labored," 4:10; but these can well be sifted and reduced in number and importance. Happily the book may be dated late if necessary.

VI

CRITICISM OF MICAH

The prophecies of Micah are woefully dismembered by modern critics. Only chaps. 1-3 are allowed to be his; and even in these, 2:12, 13

are rejected. Chapters 4-7 with great confidence
are said, by some, to give proof of exilic or post-
exilic origin (cf. 4:6, 7, 10, 11; 7:11). In no
part of chaps. 4-7 can Cheyne detect the hand of
Micah; and of the same chapters McFadyen says,
"Many elements could not possibly be Micah's."
Wellhausen, Nowack, Giesebrecht, and others, admit only a small genuine kernel; others, like Stade,
Cornill and Marti, reject this also. The alleged
"Deuteronomic coloring" is of little weight, however, being found even in Babylonian and Egyptian
prophecies as early as the second millennium B. C.
And the "abruptness," "want of connection," and
"desultoriness" of these prophecies are characteristic features of all eschatological style. Sellin regards
chaps. 4-5 as "a document of the pre-exilic eschatology of salvation," by which the prophet "shows
how Micah regarded the approaching peril of the
year 701 B. C., in the light of eschatology." The
two psalms in 7:8-20 on the subject of Zion's redemption, however, Sellin dates as either "from the
Exilic period, or from just after the Exile"; but,
Wildeboer, von Ryssel, von Orelli, Elhorst, and
Driver are content to give the entire book, with
trifling exceptions as interpolations, to Micah; while
G. A. Smith observes that "those who have recently
written the fullest monographs on Micah incline to
believe in the genuineness of the book as a whole";
and Mackay concludes that "there is no good reason
to doubt the authenticity of any part of Micah."
The fact that a prophecy of restoration, such as
2:12, 13, follows a vision of judgment is not a sufficient cause for its excision; for, as we have seen in
the cases of Hosea and Amos, judgment naturally

brings about reformation. Besides, at best we have
but a brief epitome, probably, of Micah's sermons.
To treat, indeed, as a gloss, even a phrase like "to
Babylon" in 4:10, is unnecessary in the light of
II Chron. 33:11, which reads, "The king of *Assyria*
took Manasseh in chains, and bound him with fet-
ters, and carried him to Babylon" (cf. Isa. 39:6).

VII

THE UNITY OF NAHUM

The book opens with an exordium, poetic in
character and alphabetic in form (1:2-10). Its
acrostic structure is somewhat mutilated (cf.
Psalms 9 and 10); but "there are no historical
grounds for doubting the genuineness of the psalm"
(Sellin). Numerous attempts have been made to
reconstruct it, but all have failed. As A. B.
Davidson long years ago concluded, the reconstruction of the original acrostic poem "can never
be more than an academic exercise." Dr. J. D.
Davis, however, with praiseworthy originality, has
pointed out that the prophet allowed certain con-
secutive Hebrew sounds to introduce topics rather
than sentences; thus, in the first part of the poem,
vss. 2-8, in which he describes Jehovah as over-
throwing wickedness, he employs predominatingly the first half of the letters composing the
Hebrew alphabet; whereas, in the second part of
the poem, vss. 9-15, which shows the uselessness
of opposing Him, he uses for the most part the

letters of the last part of the Hebrew alphabet. A few critics attribute the poem to a foreign source; J. M. P. Smith thinks it was "found ready at hand and forced into this service by some editor who failed to appreciate its acrostic form." G. B. Gray assigns it an origin after the Exile. Gunkel, in 1893, was really the first to assert its independence. He did so on the ground that the acrostic form was too mechanical and artificial for a poet of Nahum's freshness and vigor, and that its thought is too theological and too abstract. But it is perfectly obvious that the Book of Nahum is uniformly the same throughout, being composed of one continuous utterance and the product of one single inspiration; that, while there is a slight difference in the tone and form of the first chapter from the rest, the language and the atmosphere of the prologue are those of the succeeding oracles, and that they are all knit together by one and the same theme; in short, that the book is one organic whole.

VIII·

THE INTEGRITY OF HABAKKUK

The book by some has been needlessly dissected. Von Gumpach, in 1860, was the first to fancy he found in it a combination of two distinct prophets. De Goeje, in 1861, came independently to the same conclusion. Stade, in 1884, is credited with detaching chap. 3. Giesebrecht, in 1890, and Wellhausen, in 1892, carried the process of dissection into the

minutiæ. Marti, in 1904, reduced the compass of
Habakkuk's genuine prophecies to 1:5-10, 14ff.
Nicolardot, in 1908, contended Habakkuk wrote not
more than 2:5-9. Budde's theory is most original.
He claims that the prophet originally had in mind
the Assyrians, and that his prophecy was only subsequently accommodated to the Chaldeans. He would
read his genuine prophecies in the following order:
1:2-4, 12-17; 2:1-4; 1:6-11; 2:5-20.

The song in chap. 3 is generally rejected by
critics, but in reply it may be said: (1) That chap.
3 is the prophetic vindication of the truth of chap.
2:4b. (2) That it is most vitally connected with,
and essential to, chaps. 1-2. The last words of the
fifth woe on the Chaldeans (2:20) anticipate just
such a theophany as that described in the poem.
(3) That, whether chap. 3 belongs to Habakkuk
or not, its picture of the intervention of God himself bringing to nought all the counsels of his enemies is a most fitting close to the book. (4) That
the whole book forms a perfectly artistic whole
which may well have been given to Israel at one
time.

The following authorities maintain the genuineness of chap. 3, and, indeed, the integrity of the
entire book: Pusey, König, Ewald, Sinker, Kirkpatrick, von Orelli, and Katwijk, who in his doctor's
thesis at Amsterdam (1912) ably defends the unity
of the whole.

IX

UNITY AND INTEGRITY OF ZEPHANIAH

Of late years Zephaniah's prophecies have been the object of "an exaggerated criticism." Certain scholars, notably Stade, Wellhausen, Schwally, Budde, Cornill, G. A. Smith, McFadyen, Gray, Moore, Selbie, and J. M. P. Smith, propose to deprive the prophet of everything from 2:4 onward. Not all, however, go to this length in the process of disintegration. Cornill, for example, feels that chap. 2 is "indispensable," as forming the continuation of chap. 1. Others see that a threat against Nineveh, such as that found in 2:13-15, would sound very strange coming from a date long subsequent to the year 606, or 611 B.C., when Nineveh fell. G. A. Smith, having already cut off the promissory conclusion to the Book of Amos (Amos 9:11-15), feels it necessary to cut off also the more hopeful and peaceful epilogue in Zeph. 3:14-20; and with Selbie explains this section as having probably been introduced into its present place "to relieve a sombre background"; while J. M. P. Smith boldly claims that "Old Testament books were all subject to this kind of growth," i.e., post-exilic editors often injected messages of hope and promise into earlier oracles of threatening and despair. But, as we have observed in the cases of others, "the prophets do not usually content themselves with bare threats and announcements of judgment; neither do they ever contemplate a complete destruction of the people. The purpose of the judgment is not to exterminate but to purify."

König accepts the entire book as genuine, except the title. Driver in the earlier editions of his *Introduction* never hints that any part of the book is in dispute. Robertson Smith, writing for the *Encyclopædia Britannica* on the Book of Zephaniah, concludes, "The genuineness and integrity of the short prophecy ascribed to Zephaniah do not seem to be open to reasonable doubt. Though the sequence of thought is not so smooth as a Western reader may desire, a single leading motive runs through the whole, and the first two chapters would be incomplete without the third." And Elmslie very wisely observes, "The Book of Zephaniah is evidently an organic whole, put together on a single occasion, though of course it may sum up the teaching of a protracted ministry."

X

CRITICISM AND DATE OF HAGGAI

The critical questions involved in the case of Haggai are not serious; the genuineness and integrity of his book never being doubted really till about 1888, when Böhme cast suspicions on 1:13 and all of 2:20-23. In 1893 M. Tony André also questioned 2:10-19; but the few occasional attempts to detect secondary elements in Haggai have all proved quite unsuccessful, having found little or no acceptance.

Though written in the third person, there is little doubt but that the book is a literary unity, springing, as it states, from the second year of Darius Hystaspes, 520 B.C.; and though 1:15 is loosely connected with its context, and 2:9 has appended to it in the Greek the words, "and peace of soul for a possession to everyone who founds and raises up this temple anew"; and 2:14, also, has added to it in the Greek, "Ye hated them that reprove in the gate," there is really no ground for challenging the integrity of the book as a whole. Klostermann and Marti are quite alone in denying the book in its entirety to Haggai.

XI

CRITICAL PROBLEM IN ZECHARIAH

The unity of Zechariah's book has long been disputed. The first to question its genuineness was Joseph Mede, of Cambridge, who in 1653, out of reverence for Scripture, argued that chapters 9-11 were written by Jeremiah, because Matthew, in quoting Zech. 11:13, ascribes it to Jeremiah (cf. Matt. 27:9). But Mede's hypothesis was quite unnecessary, and was never acceptable to many. On the other hand, for half a century past two rival schools of criticism have held the field: one insisting that chapters 9-14 are pre-exilic, and the other that they are post-Zecharian. Both schools excerpt the section (13:7-9), and attach it to chapters 9-11. Of the two, the post-Zecharian is at the present time the more popular. In any case, only chapters 9-14 are in dispute, for no one doubts the genuineness of chapters 1-8.

The *pre-exilic* hypothesis we discuss first. According to those who hold this view, chapters 9-11 with 13:7-9 were uttered by a prophet in the eighth century B.C., perhaps by "Zechariah, the son of Jeberechiah," mentioned in Isa. 8:2; whereas chapters 12-14 (excepting 13:7-9) were spoken by a probable contemporary of Jeremiah, shortly before the downfall of Jerusalem in 586 B.C. It is argued that certain historical allusions in these oracles confirm this hypothesis, for example:

1. *The names given to the Theocracy:* "Ephraim" and "Jerusalem" (9:10), "Judah" and "Ephraim" (9:13); "house of Judah" and "house of Joseph" (10:6); "Judah and Israel" (11:14), which most naturally imply that the divided kingdoms of Israel and Judah were still standing when these oracles were uttered. But Zechariah himself in 8:13 (which is undisputed) addresses the "house of Israel" and the "house of Judah" in like manner; and it was quite in keeping with the custom in post-exilic times for the Jews to think of themselves as representatives of the whole twelve tribes, for they offered twelve sacrifices in Ezra's day (cf. Ezra 6:17; 8:35), and continued to reckon their genealogies tribally distinct from one another, e.g., Anna, of the tribe of Asher (Luke 2:36). Moreover, the ancient names "Israel" and "Judah" would naturally remain precious in Jewish memory.

2. *The "three shepherds" who were "cut off in one month"* (11:8) are by the advocates of the pre-exilic hypothesis identified with the three kings of North Israel, Zechariah, Shallum and Menahem,

who reigned each but a short time (cf. II Kings 15:8-15). But this identification fails, inasmuch as these three kings were not cut off "in one month"; on the contrary, Menahem reigned ten years (II Kings 15 : 17).

3. *The "great mourning in Jerusalem as the mourning of Hadadrimmon in the valley of Megiddon"* (12:11), which naturally alludes to the killing of Josiah by Pharaoh-necho at Megiddo in 609 B.C. (II Kings 23:29, 30; II Chron. 35:22-25). But the death of this last good king of Judah might easily have been remembered for more than a quarter of a century!

4. *Likewise, the earthquake in Uzziah's time,* mentioned in Zech. 14:5, does not prove the early origin of this oracle; for, if an earthquake occurring about 750 B.C., could be remembered and cited on the eve of the Exile in 586 B.C., as is claimed, it might also have been remembered still in post-exilic times.

5. *The geographical limitations of Judah, "from Geba to Rimmon"* (Zech. 14: 10), define the area occupied by the nation not only just before the captivity, but equally well the territory occupied by the Jewish colonists immediately after their return.

6. *Of greater value are the references to Israel's national sins,* which seem to have prevailed as the prophet spoke, such as idolatry, teraphim, and false prophecy (10:2; 13:2-6); these were the sins especially of pre-exilic times. But the same sins persisted in the post-exilic congregation (cf. Neh. 6:7-14; Mal. 2:11; 3:5). In any case, the prophet lays but little emphasis upon them.

7. *A still stronger argument is the mention of*

Israel's enemies as "Assyria" and "Egypt" (10:10, 11), and the cities of Syria, Phœnicia, and Philistia (9:1-7). But national names are slow to change, for example, the name "Assyria" occurs in lieu of "Babylonia" in Lam. 5:6, and "Assyria" for "Persia" in Ezra 6:22. Besides, Jeremiah prophesied against Damascus and Hamath long after their loss of independence (Jer. 49:23-27); and the Philistines of Ashdod are among those who resisted Israel's restoration of Jerusalem in the days of Nehemiah (cf. Neh. 4:7, 8). In fact, all these peoples were Israel's hereditary foes, and their old names sufficiently identified them.

In short, it may be affirmed, in opposition to the pre-exilic hypothesis, that it is perfectly obvious throughout Zechariah, chaps. 9-14, that the Exile is treated as an event of the past (9:8-11; 10:6, 8-10). Add to this the negative circumstance that the alleged authors of these oracles dissociate themselves from any definitely named person, or any specific event as transpiring when these prophecies were supposedly uttered, and the demonstration that they are of post-exilic origin ought to be complete. There is no king mentioned as ruling; God alone is described as the ruler of his people (14:9). The "house of David," mentioned in 12:7-12; 13:1, is not spoken of as in possession of the throne. Rather, it is David's *house,* and not any earthly ruler in it, of which the prophet speaks. Furthermore, there is no clear note of alarm or warning uttered in these oracles, as so frequently are found in the prophecies of Amos and Hosea, or Jeremiah. On the contrary, judgment gives place to hope, warning to encouragement, and threatening to joy

and gladness, which *ex hypothesi* is most incongru-
ous with the thought that these prophecies are of
pre-exilic stamp.

The other hypothesis remaining to be examined is
that known as the *post-Zecharian*. This is the
popular critical view at the present time. Some,
like Sellin, have in recent years shifted to this from
the pre-exilic view. Says Sellin: "I myself formerly
attributed chaps. 9-11 to a contemporary of Jeremiah, and saw in chap. 14 a post-exilic apocalyptic
addition, but my present view is that the whole work
is derived from an apocalyptic writer of the third
century B.C., who, however, wrote in the character
of a pre-exilic prophet" (*Introduction to the Old
Testament,* 1923, p. 190). The majority of critics
since Stade in 1881 have placed the origin of these
oracles in the Greek period, in the time of the
Diadochi who divided Alexander's empire, or of the
Maccabees. They rest their case for the most part
on one single passage (9:13), which mentions the
"sons of Javan," i.e., the Ionians, as the opponents
of Ephraim. Kuiper in summing up his reasons for
a late post-Zecharian date, throws the whole weight
of his argument in favor of a Greek origin on this
verse. Wellhausen makes it decide the date of these
prophecies; while Stade declares that the announcement of the "sons of Javan" in 9:13 is alone sufficient to prove that these oracles are after 333 B.C.
The features of this passage especially emphasized
are: (1) that the sons of Javan are *the* world-power
of the author's day; and (2) that they are the
enemies of Zion.

But, in opposition to these claims, it should be
observed, first, that this phrase, "sons of Javan,"

is textually confessedly in dispute and by many regarded as a gloss (cf. the LXX and Targum); that the "sons of Javan" are but one of several world-powers within the range of the prophet's horizon (9: 1-7; 12: 2 ff.; 14: 2 ff.; 10:10, 11); and that the Greeks under Alexander the Great were not enemies of Zion, and did not fight against the Jews, but against the Persians. On the other hand, assuming the genuineness of the passage, the following considerations point to the Persian period as its probable historical background: (a) the prophecy would be vague and almost meaningless if uttered *after* the invasion of Alexander; (b) the passage and its context do not describe a victory for the sons of Javan, but rather a defeat; (c) the announcement is introduced by an appeal to those still in Exile to return, which would have been quite meaningless after Alexander's conquest; (d) in short, 9:13-17, as a whole, is not a picture of actual war, but rather an apocalyptic vision of the struggle of Israel with the world-power of the West,—hence, its indefiniteness and figurative language. The real question, therefore, is, Which period would suggest such a vision? Historically, it is well known that the Greeks were rapidly becoming a menacing world-power in the first three years of Darius' reign (521-519 B.C.). During this brief period at least twelve different revolts took place, principally in the north and east. But in 518 B.C., Darius was compelled to move westward at the head of his royal armies. His visit to Egypt in 517 B.C. was cut short by the disturbances of the Greeks (Wiedermann, *Geschichte*, p. 236). In the year 516 B.C. the Greeks of the Hellespont and Bosphorus, with the

island of Samos, were made to submit to Persian
rule. During the next year, 515 B.C., Darius led an
expedition against the Scythians across the Danube,
the failure of which encouraged the Ionians subsequently to revolt. In 500 B.C. the great Ionian
revolt, so long feared, actually took place. In
409 B.C., Sardis, the most important stronghold for
Persia in Asia Minor, was burned by the Athenians.
In 490 B.C. Marathon was fought and Persia was
conquered. In 480 B.C. Xerxes was defeated at
Salamis, etc.; but it is unnecessary to sketch the rise
of Javan further. Enough has been related to show
that already in the reign of Darius Hystaspis, when
Zechariah lived and preached, the sons of Javan
were a rising and threatening world-power. This
is all, really, that is required by the passage under
examination. The sons of Javan were but one of
Israel's possible foes; but they were of such importance that victory over them, the prophet saw,
carried with it momentous messianic interests. The
language of the seer is too vague, in our judgment,
to have been uttered after Marathon, 490 B.C., or
even after the burning of Sardis, 500 B.C.; for, in
that case, the prophet would have been influenced
more by the victories of Greece and less by the
movements and commotions of other nations.

Other passages interpreted by the post-Zecharian
school in confirmation of their hypothesis are:

1. Chapter 14:9: "And Jehovah shall be king
over all the earth: in that day shall Jehovah be one,
and his name one." To Stade this passage contains
a polemic against the conditions in Greek times
when all gods were conceived of as only different
representations of one and the same god. But, on

the contrary, the post-exilic congregation was as truly a theocracy in the days of Darius Hystaspis as in the Greek period subsequent to Alexander's conquest. The Jewish colony of the Restoration from the first was a religious sect, not a political organization. Zechariah himself pictures the close relation of Jehovah to his people (2:10-13; 8:3, 23). The "yearning for a fuller theocracy," which Cheyne (*Bampton Lectures,* p. 120) discovers in Zech. 9-14, is thoroughly consistent with the yearning of a struggling congregation in a land of forsaken idols shortly after the return of Israel from Exile.

2. Chapter 12:2b is interpreted to mean that Judah also, forced by the enemy, shall be in the siege against Jerusalem, and that, therefore, the children of the Diaspora were compelled to serve as soldiers. Accordingly, this verse is interpreted as a description of the hostile relations which actually existed between Judah and Jerusalem in the beginning of the Maccabean struggle. But a correct exegesis of this passage completely refutes such a claim. The text, however, is obviously corrupt. In order to obtain a subject for the verb "shall be" the preposition before Judah would better be stricken, as in the Targum. The passage then translated reads: "And Judah also shall be in the siege against Jerusalem." But this still leaves the passage ambiguous. It may mean that Judah shall help besiege Jerusalem, or it may mean that Judah, too, like Jerusalem, shall be besieged. The latter is more probably the intended meaning as vs. 7 shows; for, as one nation might besiege a city, so all nations, coming up, are going to besiege Judah. The Septuagint

Version favors this interpretation; and likewise the Coptic (cf. Zech. 14:14). Wellhausen concedes that "no characteristic of the prophecy under discussion in reality agrees with the conditions of the Maccabean time. The Maccabees were not the Jews of the low land, and they did not join themselves with the heathen out of hatred to the city of Jerusalem, in order finally to fall treacherously upon their companions in war. There is not the slightest hint in our passage of religious persecution; that alone abides, and hence the most important sign of Maccabean times is wanting."

3. Another argument is the mention of "Egypt" and "Assyria" in 10:10, 11; which is, singularly enough, interpreted to refer, respectively, to the Ptolemies of Egypt and the Seleucidæ of Syria. But this is too far-fetched, and only begs the question.

4. Still another argument advanced in favor of a late post-Zecharian date for these oracles is that from language and style: for example, the Aramaisms, the shorter form of the Hebrew personal pronoun "I," the frequent use of the sign of the accusative, especially with suffixes, the omission of the article, and the use of the infinitive absolute, etc.— all of which, however, count for little in so brief a prophecy!

The book need not be divided. The deeper we go the nearer we approach to unity. W. E. Barnes, who divides the book, makes a fatal concession to this effect, when he allows that "Zechariah the disciple (i.e., the alleged author of chaps. 9-14) delivers the same general message as Zechariah the prophet, only under different forms" (*Camb. Bible*, p. xxi). In like manner, G. A. Smith's argument against Graetz, who divides Hosea, chaps. 1-3, from Hosea, chaps. 4-14, applies with equal fairness to Zechariah, chaps. 1-8, and Zechariah, chaps. 9-14: "In both sections not only are the religious principles identical, and many of the characteristic expressions, but there breathes throughout the same urgent and jealous temper" (*The Twelve Prophets,* I, 212). This is preëminently true of Zechariah. Certain religious and psychological peculiarities are especially noteworthy.

1. *An unusually deep spiritual tone pervades the entire book.* The prophet's introductory call to true repentance, first sounded forth in 1:1-7, is developed and emphasized in a variety of ways throughout the entire book, thus, in the sanctifying of Joshua (3:4), in Jehovah's message to Zerubbabel, "not by might nor by power, but by my spirit" (4:6), in the obedience demanded as a condition precedent of future blessing (6:15), in the answer made by the prophet to the Bethel deputation concerning fasting (7:5-9; 8:16ff.), in the consecration of the remnant of the Philistines (9:7), in the blessings promised to Ephraim (10:12), in the baptism of grace upon Jerusalem (12:10), in the fountain provided for sin and for uncleanness (13:1), in the worship of Jehovah by the purified remnant of Israel (13:9), in the living waters going forth from Jerusalem (14:8), and in the dedication of everything as holy unto Jehovah (14:20, 21). Thus, the tone which everywhere tempers these prophecies is an extraordinarily deep and spiritual one throughout. Indeed, the passages here cited in proof of this claim are the really characteristic pas-

sages of the book in both its parts, and must not be deleted arbitrarily as is done by some.

2. *A pronounced attitude of hope and expectation also dominates the prophecies throughout.* This, too, is especially characteristic. Such an optimism would naturally accompany the building of God's house to its final completion. For example, the return of the whole nation to the Holy Land is a prevailing idea and source of happiness and joy in both parts (2:6, 10; 8:7, 8; 9:12; 10:6, 7); and especially the fact that "many nations shall join themselves to Jehovah in that day" (2:11; 6:15; 8:23; 14:16. This spirit of optimism which pervades the whole book of Zechariah is most remarkable. But not less noteworthy is the position of importance which the Temple occupies. When it is completed it is expected to become the center of the nation's religious life (1:16, 17; 3:7; 6:15; 7:2, 3; 9:8; 14:20). Messianic hope is peculiarly strong and conspicuous (3:8, 9; 6:12, 13; 9:9, 10; 11:12, 13; 12:10; 13:1, 7-9, for all these passages, whatever their origin, transcend their local horizon in the sense that they find their fulfilment first in Jesus Christ. In like manner, peace and prosperity are also expected as accompaniments of Temple construction (1:17; 3:10; 6:13; 8:12, 19; 9:10, 12, 17; 10:1, 7, 8, 10, 12; 12:8; 14:11, cf. vss. 16-19).

3. *And the idea of God's providence as extending over the whole earth* is another dominant thought (1:14-17; 2:9, 12; 12:2-4, 8; 13:7; 14:3, 9).

4. *So, also, Jehovah's attitude toward Judah and Jerusalem:* in both parts it is an attitude of supreme regard for Judah's interests, which are second only to those of the capital itself (1:12; 2:2, 4, 12; 5:3;

8 :3, 13, 15, 19; 9 :9, 13; 10 :3, 6; 11 :14; 12 :2, 4, 6, 7; 13 :1; 14 :2, 14, 21).

5. *Besides all these, there are peculiarities of thought common to both parts,* which psychologically bind the whole book together as the expression of one mind: for example (a) the habit of dwelling on the same thought repeatedly (2 :10, 15; 6 :12, 13; 8 : 21, 22 : 11 : 7; 13 : 3; 14 : 5, 16, 18, 19) ; (b) the habit of expanding one fundamental thought into a series of clauses (1 :17; 3 :8, 9; 6 :12, 13; 9 :5-7; 14 :4) ; (c) especially the habit of referring to a thought already introduced, e.g., "Branch" (3 :8; 6 :12) ; "eyes" (3 : 9; 4 :10) ; "measuring line" (1 : 16; 2 :1) ; "choose Jerusalem" (1 :17; 2 :12; 3 :2) ; "remove the iniquity" (3 :9; 5 :3, 4; 13 :2) ; disposition to measure distances (2 :1; 5 :2; 14 :10) ; colors of horses (1 : 8; 6 : 2, 3, 6) ; the idea of Israel as a "flock" (9 :16; 10 :2; 11 :4, 7, 17) ; idols (10 :2; 13 :2) ; and many "nations" (2 :11; 8 :23; 11 :10; 12 :3; 14 :2) ; (d) the use made of the cardinal number "two", thus, "two olive trees" (4 :3) ; "two women" (5 :9), "two mountains" (6 :1), "two staves" (11 :7), and "two halves" (14 :2, 4, 8) ; with which compare also 6 :13 and 9 :12; (e) likewise, the use made, in both parts of the book, of symbolic actions as a mode of instruction, e.g., the coronation scene in 6 :9-15, and the breaking of the two staves in 11 :4-14.

6. *Certain peculiarities of diction and style also favor unity of authorship,* e.g., (a) the phrase, "that none pass through or return" (7 :14; 9 :8) is a combination of Hebrew words never elsewhere occurring in the entire Old Testament; (b) the author's preference for and frequent use of voca-

tives (2:7, 10, 13; 3:2, 8; 4:7; 9:9, 12, 13; 11:1, 2; 13:7); and (c) the frequent alternation of the *scriptio plena* and the *scripto defectiva* in Hebrew (1:2, 5, compared with 1:4, 6, and 8:14; also 9:5 with 10:5, 11; and 9:9 with 10:4).

The logical conclusion from all these data seems to be that Zechariah, chaps. 9-14, are of post-exilic origin, though not necessarily post-Zecharian; and that they were all probably written by Zechariah himself during the period just prior to the completion of the Temple in 516 B.C. Besides, if composed by other prophets either earlier or later, one wonders how they came to be appended by the collectors of the Canon to the genuine prophecies of Zechariah!